D0447388

Pocket Handbook of

CHRISTIAN APOLOGETICS

PETER KREEFT
AND RONALD K. TACELLI

InterVarsity Press
Downers Grove, Illinois

InterVarsity Press
P.O. Box 1400, Downers Grove, IL 60515-1426
World Wide Web: www.ivpress.com
E-mail: email@ivpress.com

InterVarsity Press® is the book-publishing division of InterVarsity Christian Fellowship/USA®, a student movement active on campus at hundreds of universities, colleges and schools of nursing in the United States of America, and a member movement of the International Fellowship of Evangelical Students. For information about local and regional activities, write Public Relations Dept., InterVarsity Christian Fellowship/USA, 6400 Schroeder Rd., P.O. Box 7895, Madison, WI 53707-7895, or visit the IVCF website at <www.intervarsity.org>.

This edition is abridged and revised from Handbook of Christian Apologetics, *copyright 1994 by Peter Kreeft and Ronald K. Tacelli.*

Cover design: Cindy Kiple

Cover image: Jules Frazier/Getty Images

ISBN-10: 0-8308-2702-1
ISBN-13: 978-0-8308-2702-2

Printed in the United States of America ∞

Library of Congress Cataloging-in-Publication Data

Kreeft, Peter.
Pocket handbook of Christian apologetics/ Peter Kreeft and Ronald K. Tacelli.
p.cm
Rev. ed. of: Handbook of Christian apologetics. 1994.
Includes bibliographical references and index.
ISBN 0-8308-2702-1 (pbk.: alk. paper)
1. Apologetics. I. Tacelli, Ronald K. (Ronald Keith), 1947- II. Kreeft, Peter. Handbook of Christian apologetics. III. Title.
BT1103.K725 2003
239—dc21 *2003006757*

P 18 17 16 15 14 13 12 11 10 9 8 7 6
Y 17 16 15 14 13 12 11 10 09 08

To Cyndi and Rich—

what more could a brother ask for?

To John Kreeft

who had a large role in shaping this book

and a larger role in shaping

one of its authors

Contents

1

Apologetics

"Be ready to give a reason for the hope that is in you" (1 Pet 3:15). Apologetics is the enterprise of obeying that command.

Reasons for Apologetics

Many people scorn apologetics because it seems very intellectual, abstract and rational. They contend that life and love and morality and sanctity are much more important than reason.

Those who reason this way are right; they just don't notice that they are *reasoning*. We can't avoid reasoning; we can only avoid doing it well.

Further, reason is a friend to faith (see chapter two).

Another, deeper reason why some people scorn apologetic reasoning is that they decide with their hearts much more than with their heads whether to believe or not. The heart *is* our center, not the head. But apologetics gets at the heart *through* the head. The head is important precisely because it is a gate to the heart. We can love only what we know.

Further, reason at least has veto power. We can't believe what we believe to be untrue, and we can't love what we believe to be unreal. Arguments may not bring you to faith, but they can certainly keep you away from faith. Therefore we must join the battle of arguments.

Arguments can bring you closer to faith in the same sense that a car can bring you to the sea. The car can't swim; you have to jump in to do that. But you can't jump in from a hundred miles inland. You need a car first to bring you to the point where you can make a leap of faith into the sea. Faith is a leap, but a leap in the light, not in the dark.

We invite critics, skeptics, unbelievers and believers in other religions to dialogue with us and write to us—for the sake of our mutual pursuit of truth and for the (much less important) sake of improving future editions of this book. One of the few things in life that cannot possibly do harm in the end is the honest pursuit of the truth.

Concerning Methodology

An introduction to apologetics usually deals with methodology. We do not. We believe that nowadays second-order questions of method often distract attention from first-order questions of truth. Our intent is to get "back to basics." We have no particular methodological ax to grind. We try to use commonsense standards of rationality and universally agreed principles of logic in all our arguing.

But we must say one thing about method: argumentation is a human enterprise that is embedded in a larger social and psychological context. This context includes (1) the total psyches of the two persons engaged in dialogue, (2) the relationship between the two persons, (3) the immediate situation in which they find themselves and (4) the larger social, cultural and historical situation surrounding them. Even national, political, racial and sexual factors influence the apologetic situation. One should not use the same arguments in discussion with a Muslim woman from Tehran that one would use with an African American teenager from Los Angeles.

In other words, arguments are more like swords than bombs. It matters little who drops a bomb. But it matters enormously who wields a sword, for a sword is an extension of the swordsman. Thus, an argument in apologetics, when actually used in dialogue, is an extension of the arguer. The arguer's tone, sincerity, care, concern, listening and respect matter as much as his or her logic—probably more. The world was won for Christ not by arguments but by sanctity: "What you are speaks so loud, I can hardly hear what you say."

The Need for Apologetics Today

Apologetics is especially needed today, when the world stands at a triple crossroads and crisis.

Western civilization is for the first time in its history in danger of dying. The reason is spiritual. It is losing its life, its soul; that soul was the Christian faith. The infection killing it is not multiculturalism—other faiths—but the monoculturalism of secularism—no faith, no soul. The twentieth century has been marked by genocide, sexual chaos and money-worship. Unless all the prophets are liars, we are doomed unless we repent and "turn back the clock" (not technologically but spiritually).

We are not only in a civil, cultural crisis but also in a philosophical, intellectual one. Our crisis is "a crisis of truth" (to use Ralph Martin's title). Increasingly, the very idea of objective truth is being ignored, abandoned or attacked—especially by the educational and media establishments, who mold our minds. (See chapter fifteen for a defense of objective truth.)

The deepest level of our crisis is not cultural or intellectual but spiritual. At stake are the eternal souls of men and women for whom Christ died. Some think the end is near. We are skeptical of such predictions, but we know one thing with certainty: our civilization may last for another century, but you will not. You will soon stand naked in the light of God. You had better learn to love and seek that light while there is still time, so that it will be your joy and not your fear forever. It is unfashionable today to put such things in print—a fact that says volumes about the spiritual sanity of our ostrichlike age.

Mere, or Orthodox, Christianity

We confine ourselves in this book to the core beliefs common to all orthodox Christians—what C. S. Lewis called "mere Christianity." By *mere* we do not mean some abstract "lowest common denominator," but the heart or essence of the faith, as summarized in the Apostles' Creed. This ancient and unchanging core unites diverse believers with each other and against unbelievers within many churches and denominations as well as without. Liberal (or modernist or demythologist or revisionist) theologians will not like this book, especially its arguments for miracles, the reliability of Scripture, the reality of the resurrection, the divinity of Christ and the reality of heaven and hell. We invite them to join the self-confessed unbelievers in trying to refute these arguments. We also invite them to begin practicing more accurate "truth in labeling" in describing their own position.

2

Faith and Reason

In a sense the marriage of faith and reason is the most important question in apologetics because it is the overall question. If faith and reason are incompatible, then apologetics is impossible. For apologetics is the attempt to defend faith with reason's weapons.

Defining *Faith*

We must distinguish the *act* of faith from the *object* of faith, believing from what is believed.

The object of faith means all the things believed. For the Christian, this means everything God has revealed in the Bible; Catholics include all the creeds and universal binding teachings of the Church as well. This faith (the object, not the act) is expressed in propositions.

Propositions are many, but the ultimate object of faith is one. The ultimate object of faith is not words but God's Word (singular)—indeed, God himself. Without a living relationship to the living God, propositions are pointless, for their point is to point beyond themselves to God. ("A finger is good for pointing to the moon, but woe to him who mistakes the finger for the moon," according to a wise Zen saying.) But without propositions, we cannot know or tell others what God we believe in and what we believe about God.

The act of *faith* is more than merely an act of *belief.* We believe many things—for example, that the Lakers will beat the Celtics, that the President is not a crook, that Norway is beautiful—but we are not willing to die for these beliefs, nor can we live them every moment. But religious faith is something to die for and something to live every moment. It is much more than belief, and much stronger, though belief is one of its parts or aspects.

We can distinguish at least four aspects or dimensions of religious faith.

1. Emotional faith is feeling assurance or trust or confidence in a person. This includes hope (which is much stronger than just a wish) and peace (which is much stronger than mere calm).

2. Intellectual faith is belief. It is this aspect of faith that is formulated in propositions and summarized in creeds.

3. Volitional faith is an act of the will, a commitment to obey God's will. This faith is faithfulness, or fidelity. It manifests itself in behavior, that is, in good works.

4. Faith begins in that obscure mysterious center of our being that Scripture calls the "heart." *Heart* in Scripture does not mean feeling or sentiment or emotion, but the absolute center of the soul, as the physical heart is at the center of the body.

"Keep your heart with all vigilance," advised Solomon, "for from it flow the springs of life" (Prov 4:23). With the heart we choose our "fundamental option" of yes or no to God, and thereby determine our eternal identity and destiny.

Defining *Reason*

Here again we must distinguish the subjective, personal *act* of reason from the *object* of reason.

The object of reason means all that reason can know. This means all the truths that can be (a) *understood* by human reason, (b) *discovered* by human reason and (c) *proved* by reason without any premises assumed by faith in divine revelation.

Reason is relative to truth; it is a way of knowing truth: understanding it, discovering it or proving it. Faith is also relative to truth; it too is a way of discovering truth. No human being ever existed without some faith. We all know most of what we know by faith; that is, by belief in what others—parents, teachers, friends, writers, society—tell us. Outside religion as well as inside it, faith *and* reason are roads to truth.

The Relation Between the Objects of Faith and Reason

Having defined our two terms, we are ready to ask the question about the relation between them. When we ask this question, we do not mean "What is the *psychological* relation between the *act* of faith and the *act* of reason?" but "What is the *logical* relation between the *object* of faith and the *object* of reason?" How are these two sets of truths—those knowable by unaided human reason and those knowable by faith in divine revelation—related? There are three different kinds of truths:

1. Truths of faith and not of reason
2. Truths of both faith and reason
3. Truths of reason and not of faith

Truths of faith alone are things revealed by God but not understandable, discoverable or provable by reason (e.g., the Trinity or the fact that Christ's death atoned for our sins). Truths of both faith and reason are things revealed by God but also understandable, discoverable or provable by reason (e.g., the existence of one God, or an objective moral law, or life after death). Truths of reason and not of faith are things not revealed by God but known by human reason (e.g., the natural sciences). If this is the correct position, it follows that the Christian apologist has two tasks: to prove all the propositions in class *2* and to answer all objections to the propositions in class *1* (see figure 1).

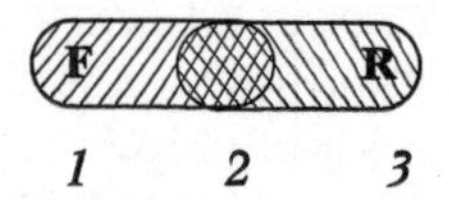

Figure 1

We cannot prove the propositions in class *1* (e.g., the Trinity), but we can answer all objections to them. For example, suppose a Unitarian or a Muslim objects to the Trinity because "it is polytheistic." We can show that this is a misunderstanding; it does not mean three Gods, but one God in three Persons. Or suppose a logician says it is a contradiction to call anything both one and three. We can reply that God is one nature, not three, and three persons, not one. This is not a contradiction, any more than we are: we are two natures (spirit and animal, mind and matter, soul and body) but one person.

Christian thinkers do not all agree about how many of the propositions of faith can be proved by reason, but most have held that some could (thus apologetics is possible) but not all (thus apologetics is limited).

Why Faith and Reason Can Never Contradict Each Other

Aquinas's answer to this question in *Summa Contra Gentiles* 1.7 seems to us irrefutably true:

> The truth that the human reason is naturally endowed to know cannot be opposed to the truth of the Christian faith. For that with which the human reason is naturally endowed is clearly most true; so much so, that it is impossible for us to think of such truths as false. [If we only

> understand the meaning of the terms in such self-evident propositions as "The whole is greater than the part" or "Effects must have causes," we cannot think them false.] Nor is it permissible to believe as false that which we hold by faith, since this is confirmed in a way that is so clearly divine. [It is not our faith but its object, God, that justifies our certainty.] Since, therefore, only the false is opposed to the true, as is clearly evident from an examination of their definitions, it is impossible that truth of faith should be opposed to those principles that the human reason knows naturally.

Thus, either Christianity is false, or reason is false, or—if both are true—there can never be any real contradiction at all between them, since truth cannot contradict truth.

Aquinas gives a second, equally compelling reason for the same conclusion:

> Furthermore, that which is introduced into the soul of the student by the teacher is contained in the knowledge of the teacher—unless his teaching is fictitious, which it is improper to say of God. Now the knowledge of the principles that are known to us naturally [rationally self-evident propositions] has been implanted in us by God; for God is the Author of our nature. These principles, therefore, are also contained by the divine Wisdom. Hence, whatever is opposed to them is opposed to the divine Wisdom and therefore cannot come from God. That which we hold by faith as divinely revealed, therefore, cannot be contrary to our natural knowledge.

Many will follow Aquinas so far but balk at his next point. Yet this next point follows necessarily from the previous one:

> From this we evidently gather the following conclusion: whatever arguments are brought forward against the

> doctrines of faith are conclusions incorrectly derived from the first and self-evident principles embedded in [rational human] nature. Such conclusions do not have the force of demonstration; they are arguments that are either probable or sophistical [fallacious]. And so there exists the possibility to answer them.

In other words, every possible argument against every Christian doctrine has a rational mistake in it somewhere and therefore can be answered by reason alone.

If this were not so, if Aquinas is wrong here, then one of those arguments from unbelievers against one of the doctrines of Christianity, at least, would really and truly prove the doctrine to be false, that is, prove Christianity untrue. Aquinas's optimistic view of the marriage between faith and reason necessarily follows from the simple premise that Christianity is true. Thus "Christian irrationalism" is self-contradictory.

Remember, however, that we (and Aquinas) are not claiming that all Christian doctrines can be proved by reason, only that every argument against them can be disproved. Nor are we claiming that any given person can disprove them. Reason is flawless, de jure, but reasoners are not, de facto.

3

Arguments for the Existence of God

Many people, both believers and nonbelievers, doubt that God's existence can be demonstrated or even argued about. But no one can reasonably doubt that attention to these arguments has its place in any book on apologetics. For very many have believed that such arguments are possible and that some of them actually work.

They have also believed that an effective rational argument for God's existence is an important first step in opening the mind to the possibility of faith.

You may not feel that they are particularly valuable to you. You may be blessed with a vivid sense of God's presence—something for which to be profoundly grateful. But that does not mean you have no obligation to ponder these arguments. For many have not been blessed in that way. And the proofs are designed for them—or some of them at least—to give a kind of help they really need. You may even be asked to provide that help.

The Argument from Efficient Causality

We notice that some things cause other things to be (to begin to be, to continue to be, or both). For example, a man playing the piano is causing the music that we hear. If he stops, so does the music.

Now ask yourself: Are all things caused to exist by other things right now? Suppose they are. That is, suppose there is no Uncaused Being, no God. Then nothing could exist right now. For remember, on the no-God hypothesis, all things need a present cause outside of themselves in order to exist. So right now, all things, including all those things which are causing other things to be, need a cause. They can give being only so long as they are given being. Everything that exists, therefore, on this hypothesis, stands in need of being caused to exist.

But caused by what? Beyond everything that is, there can only be nothing. But that is absurd: all of reality dependent—but dependent on nothing! The hypothesis that all being is caused, that there is no Uncaused Being, is absurd. So there must be something uncaused, something on which all things that need an efficient cause of being are dependent.

Existence is like a gift given from cause to effect. If there is no one who *has* the gift, the gift cannot be passed down the chain of receivers, however long or short the chain may be. If everyone has to borrow a certain book, but no one actually *has* it, then no one will ever *get* it. If there is no God who has existence by his own eternal nature, then the gift of existence cannot be passed down the chain of creatures and we can never get it. But we do get it; we exist. Therefore there must exist a God: an Uncaused Being who does not have to receive existence like us—and like every other link in the chain of receivers.

The Design Argument

Design arguments are of wide and perennial appeal. Almost

everyone admits that reflection on the order and beauty of nature touches something very deep within us. But are the order and beauty the products of intelligent design and conscious purpose? For theists the answer is yes. Arguments for design are attempts to vindicate this answer, to show why it is the most reasonable one to give. They have been formulated in ways as richly varied as the experience in which they are rooted. The following displays the core or central insight.

1. The universe displays a staggering amount of intelligibility, both within the things we observe and in the way these things relate to others outside themselves. That is to say: the way they exist and coexist displays an intricately beautiful order and regularity that can fill even the most casual observer with wonder. It is the norm in nature for many different beings to work together to produce the same valuable end—for example, the organs in the body work for our life and health.
2. Either this intelligible order is the product of chance or the product of intelligent design.
3. Not chance. For *less* (no order) cannot cause *more* (order).
4. Therefore the universe is the product of intelligent design.
5. Design comes only from a mind, a designer.
6. Therefore the universe is the product of an intelligent Designer.

QUESTION: *But what if the order we experience is merely a product of our minds? Even though we cannot think utter chaos and disorder, maybe that is how reality really is.*

Reply: Our minds are the only means by which we can know reality. We have no other access. If we agree that something cannot exist in thought, we cannot go ahead and say that it might nevertheless exist in reality. Then we would be thinking what we claim cannot be thought.

The *Kalām* Argument

The Arabic word *kalām* literally means "speech," but it came to denote a certain type of philosophical theology—a type containing demonstrations that the world could not be infinitely old and must therefore have been created by God. This sort of demonstration has had a long and wide appeal among both Christians and Muslims. Its form is simple and straightforward.

1. Whatever begins to exist has a cause for its coming into being.
2. The universe began to exist.
3. Therefore, the universe has a cause for its coming into being.

Grant the first premise. (Most people—outside of asylums and graduate schools—would consider it not only true but certainly and obviously true.)

Is the second premise true? Did the universe—the collection of all things bounded by space and time—begin to exist? This premise has recently received powerful support from natural science—from so-called Big Bang cosmology. But there are philosophical arguments in its favor as well. Can an infinite task ever be done or completed? If, in order to reach a certain end, infinitely many steps had to precede it, could the end ever be reached? Of course not—not even in an infinite time. For an infinite time would be unending, just as the steps would be. In other words, no end would ever be reached. The task would—could—never be completed.

If it always was, then it is infinitely old. If it is infinitely old, then an infinite amount of time would have to have elapsed before (say) today. And so an infinite number of days must have been completed—one day succeeding another, one bit of time being added to what went before—in order for the present day to arrive. But this exactly parallels the problem of an infinite task.

The Ontological Argument

The ontological argument was devised by Anselm of Canterbury (1033-1109). Most people who first hear it are tempted to dismiss it immediately as an interesting riddle, but distinguished thinkers of every age, including our own, have risen to defend it. It is the most intensely philosophical proof for God's existence; its place of honor is not within popular piety but rather textbooks and professional journals. We include it, with a minimum of discussion, not because we think it conclusive or irrefutable but for the sake of completeness.

1. It is greater for a thing to exist in the mind *and* in reality than in the mind alone.
2. *God* means "that than which a greater cannot be thought."
3. Suppose that God exists in the mind but not in reality.
4. Then a greater than God *could* be thought (namely, a being that has all the qualities our thought of God has *plus* real existence).
5. But this is impossible, for God is "that than which a greater cannot be thought."
6. Therefore God exists in the mind *and* in reality.

The Moral Argument

1. Real moral obligation is a fact. We are really, truly, objectively obligated to do good and avoid evil.
2. Either the atheistic view of reality is correct or the "religious" one is.
3. But the atheistic one is incompatible with there being moral obligation.
4. Therefore the "religious" view of reality is correct.

We need to be clear about what the first premise is claiming. It does not mean merely that we can find people around who claim to have certain duties. Nor does it mean that there have been many people who thought they were obliged to do certain things (like clothing the naked) and to avoid doing others (like committing adultery). The first premise is claiming something more: namely, that we human beings really are obligated, that our duties arise from the way things really are and not simply from our desires or subjective dispositions. It is claiming, in other words, that moral values or obligations themselves—and not merely the belief in moral values—are objective facts.

Now given the fact of moral obligation, a question naturally arises. Does the picture of the world presented by atheism accord with this fact? The answer is no. Atheists never tire of telling us that we are the chance products of the motion of matter, a motion which is purposeless and blind to every human striving. We should take them at their word and ask, Given this picture, in what exactly is the moral good rooted? Moral obligation can hardly be rooted in a material motion blind to purpose.

Suppose we say it is rooted in nothing deeper than human willing and desire. In that case, we have no moral standard against which human desires can be judged. For every desire will spring from the same ultimate source—purposeless, pitiless matter. And what becomes of obligation? According to this view, if I say there is an obligation to feed the hungry, I would be stating a fact about my wants and desires and nothing else. I would be saying that I want the hungry to be fed, and that I choose to act on that desire. But this amounts to an admission that neither I nor anyone else is really obliged to feed the hungry—that, in fact, no one has any real obligations at all. Therefore the atheistic view of reality is not compatible with there being genuine moral obligation.

The Argument from Conscience

Since moral subjectivism is very popular today, the following version of, or twist to, the moral argument should be effective, since it does not presuppose moral objectivism. Modern people often say they believe that there are no universally binding moral obligations, that we must all follow our own private conscience. But that very admission is enough of a premise to prove the existence of God.

Isn't it remarkable that no one, even the most consistent subjectivist, believes that it is ever good for anyone to deliberately and knowingly disobey his or her own conscience? Even if different people's consciences tell them to do or avoid totally different things, there remains one moral absolute for everyone: never disobey your own conscience.

Now where did conscience get such an absolute authority—an authority admitted even by the moral subjectivist and relativist? There are only four possibilities: (1) from something less than me (nature); (2) from me (individual); (3) from others equal to me (society); or (4) from something above me (God). Let's consider each of these possibilities in order.

1. How can I be absolutely obligated by something less than me—for example, by animal instinct or practical need for material survival?
2. How can I obligate myself absolutely? Am I absolute? Do I have the right to demand absolute obedience from anyone, even myself? And if I am the one who locked myself in this prison of obligation, I can also let myself out, thus destroying the absoluteness of the obligation which we admitted as our premise.
3. How can society obligate me? What right do my equals have to impose their values on me? Does quantity make quality? Do a million human beings make a relative into an absolute? Is "society" God?
4. The only source of absolute moral obligation left is something superior to me. This binds my will morally, with rightful demands for complete obedience.

Thus God, or something like God, is the only adequate source and ground for the absolute moral obligation we all feel to obey our conscience. Conscience is thus explainable only as the voice of God in the soul.

The Argument from Desire

1. Every natural, innate desire in us corresponds to some real object that can satisfy that desire.
2. But there exists in us an innate desire which nothing in time, nothing on earth, no creature can satisfy.
3. Therefore there must exist something more than time, earth and creatures that can satisfy this desire.
4. This something is what people call "God" and "life with God forever."

The first premise implies a distinction of desires into two kinds: innate and externally conditioned, or natural and artificial. We naturally desire things like food, drink, sex, sleep, knowledge, friendship and beauty; and we naturally shun things like starvation, loneliness, ignorance and ugliness. We also desire (but not innately or naturally) things like sports cars, political office, flying through the air like Superman, the land of Oz and a Red Sox world championship.

Now there are differences between these two kinds of desires. For example, we do not, for the most part, recognize corresponding states of deprivation for the second, the artificial, desires as we do for the first. There is no word like *Ozlessness* parallel to *sleeplessness.* But more important, the natural desires come from within, from our nature, while the artificial ones come from without, from society, advertising or fiction. This second difference is the reason for a third difference: the natural desires are found in all of us, but the artificial ones vary from person to person.

The existence of the artificial desires does not necessarily mean that the desired objects exist. Some do; some don't. Sports cars do; Oz does not. But the existence of natural desires does, in every discoverable case, mean that the objects desired exist. No one has ever found one case of an innate desire for a nonexistent object.

The second premise requires only honest introspection. If someone denies it and says, "I am perfectly happy playing with mud pies, or sports cars, or money, or sex, or power," we can only ask, "Are you, really?" But we can only appeal, we cannot compel. And we can refer such a person to the nearly universal testimony of human history in all its great literature. Even the atheist Jean-Paul Sartre admitted that "there comes a time when one asks, even of Shakespeare, even of Beethoven, 'Is that all there is?' "

C. S. Lewis, who uses this argument in a number of places, summarizes it succinctly:

> Creatures are not born with desires unless satisfaction for these desires exists. A baby feels hunger; well, there is such a thing as food. A duckling wants to swim; well, there is such a thing as water. Men feel sexual desire; well, there is such a thing as sex. If I find in myself a desire which no experience in this world can satisfy, the most probable explanation is that I was made for another world. (*Mere Christianity*, bk. 3, chap. 10)

The Argument from Aesthetic Experience

1. There is the music of Johann Sebastian Bach.
2. Therefore there must be a God.

You either see this one or you don't.

Pascal's Wager

Suppose you, the reader, still feel that all of these arguments are inconclusive. There is another, different kind of argument left. It has come to be known as Pascal's Wager. We mention it here and adapt it for our purposes, not because it is a proof for the existence of God but because it can help us in our search for God in the absence of such proof.

As originally proposed by Pascal, the Wager assumes that logical reasoning by itself cannot decide for or against the existence of God; there seem to be good reasons on both sides. Now since reason cannot decide for sure, and since the question is of such importance that we must decide somehow, then we must "wager" if we cannot prove. And so we are asked: Where are you going to place your bet?

If you place it with God, you lose nothing, even if it turns out that God does not exist. But if you place it against God, and you are wrong and God does exist, you lose everything: God, eternity, heaven, infinite gain. "Let us assess the two cases: if you win, you win everything; if you lose, you lose nothing" (see figure 2).

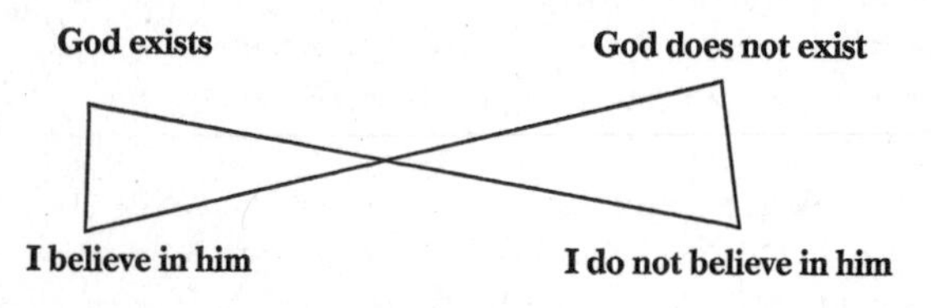

Figure 2

The Wager can seem offensively venal and purely selfish. But it can be reformulated to appeal to a higher moral motive: If there is a God of infinite goodness, and he justly deserves my allegiance and faith, I risk doing the greatest injustice by not acknowledging him.

The Wager cannot—or should not—coerce belief. But it can be an incentive for us to search for God, to study and restudy the arguments that seek to show that there is Something—or

Someone—who is the ultimate explanation of the universe and of my life. It could at lease motivate "The Prayer of the Skeptic": "God, I don't know whether you exist or not, but if you do, please show me who you are."

Pascal says that there are three kinds of people: those who have sought God and found him, those who are seeking and have not yet found, and those who neither seek nor find. The first are reasonable and happy, the second are reasonable and unhappy, the third are both unreasonable and unhappy. If the Wager stimulates us at least to seek, then it will at least stimulate us to be reasonable. And if the promise Jesus makes is true, all who seek will find (Mt 7:7-8) and, thus, will be happy.

4

The Nature of God

You may have noticed that most of the proofs presented in chapter three begin with things familiar to us—our experience of change, for example, or of living a moral life. They call to our attention certain features of these familiar things that are puzzling, certain features about which we can—and should—ask questions. Now if the questions raised in the proofs are real ones—questions like, how come the material universe exists?—if they are of a sort that admit some kind of answer, then we can see, if we reflect, that the answer is not to be found within the world of finite and familiar things. In other words, anything that answers the question is going to be of a kind altogether *unfamiliar* to us.

Language About God

If this is the case, then how can we speak of God? If God is so mysterious, how can language, which fundamentally refers to the world of our familiar experience, ever properly be used of him? This a fair question, but not a hopelessly unanswerable one, as some have thought. For it is the legitimacy of certain questions about the experienced world that allows us to think in a systematic way about God. God is the answer to these questions. He is the cause of these phenomena. And by meditating on his effects we can know *something* of their cause, shed *some* light on God himself—even though it be only a pinpoint of light.

Something similar happens in science. For example, physicists notice certain regularly occurring effects and give a name to what produces them. They have no direct observation of the causes they name, and in fact they know that some of them cannot ever be observed. But they have no trouble in calling by name what produces these effects—and even in ascribing unusual properties to such theoretical entities on the basis of their observation.

But here the similarity ends. After all, gluons and muons are part of the physical world and share its fundamental properties; God, on the other hand, is the Creator of the world. He cannot exist in the same way that the physical world exists. For as we have stressed repeatedly, it is just those properties essential to the physical world that raise the question whose answer is God. Some writers on the divine nature give the impression that God himself has sat for their portrait. We hope to create no such impression. We simply want to start from the discussion of God's existence, reflect on the demonstrations found there and ask what they imply about the One whose existence they demonstrate.

The Attributes of God

God exists absolutely. In saying "God exists absolutely" we do not mean merely that God is always there or that he does not tend to go out of existence. These things are true, in a sense. But we mean something more.

God is the source of being, or existence, for all things. Looking at the universe we see that in every creature there is a distinction between its *essence* and its *existence;* that there is a difference between *what* things are and the fact *that* they are. That is why, as we saw, limited things are by their essence alone existential zeros, why they have a need for being that they cannot themselves supply.

If God is the answer to this question about finite being, then he cannot suffer from this same need. In other words, in God there can be no such distance between *what* he is and *that* he is. That he exists is not a happy accident, not due to some other being as his cause. Being must be inseparable from what he is; it must belong to him by nature. More radically put, God must be identical with the fullness of being. That is what we mean by saying that God exists absolutely.

God is infinite. We saw that it is a finite or limited being that poses a question for us, that seems to require a condition or cause for its existence. So God cannot be limited or finite. In other words, God must be infinite, utterly limitless.

God is one. If God is infinite, can there be many Gods? Obviously not. God must exist without limit. He must be the limitless fullness of being and cannot be limited by another God outside himself. So God must be one.

God is spiritual. By saying God is spiritual, we mean that God is not a material being. To be a material being is to be a body of some kind. But a body is always limited and subject to change.

God is eternal. God cannot be subject to time, for God is the Creator of everything that changes, everything that raises a question about its own being. All beings subject to time raise that question. God cannot be like that.

The Incarnation does not contradict this; rather, it presupposes it. The Incarnation means that God took on himself, in Christ, a human nature, which included time, space and matter. This presupposes that the divine nature is different from human nature. Part of that difference has traditionally been seen as God's not being limited by time, space and matter. Only if a bird *doesn't* swim in the ocean but flies in the air can it *enter* the ocean from above; only because God is *not* temporal can he *enter* into time.

God is transcendent and immanent. God cannot be a *part* of the universe. If he were, he would be limited by other parts of it. But God is the *Creator* of all things, giving them their total being. He cannot be one of them, or the totality of them—for each one of them, and so the totality of them, must be given being, must receive being from God. So God must be *other* than his creation. This is what we mean by the *transcendence* of God.

At the same time God must be fully *present* in all things. They cannot be set over against him, for then he would be limited by them. Shakespeare was limited by his contemporaries but not by his creations; by Marlowe but not by Hamlet.

Note how this affirmation of God's transcendence and immanence avoids the one-sided pitfalls of pantheism (which identifies God with material nature) and deism (which makes God remote from creation, as if he could wind it up and let it run on its own).

God is intelligent. God is the Creator and Sustainer of all things. He is, for example, the Creator and Sustainer of all physical and chemical elements and all living organisms. Now every one of these things has an intelligible structure and fits within a system of intelligible structure. So it is reasonable to affirm that all the vast intelligibility, which the world is given by its Creator, is the work of intelligence and, therefore, that the Creator is intelligent.

God is omniscient and omnipotent. To say that God is omniscient and omnipotent means that there can be no real barriers to God's knowing or acting. Apart from himself, God has created everything there is to be known and sustains it in being. So is it conceivable that there is something he could not know or not have power over? It is impossible to think of something as thwarting God's will, unless God himself allows the thwarting—

as in the human free choice to sin. But that is a circumstance that presupposes omnipotence and therefore is not an argument against it.

But some may think that we have said too little. They see a great distance here between the loving Father revealed in Scripture and the infinitely mysterious Creator revealed in philosophical speculation. And we admit this: the kind of love revealed in Jesus is far greater than what we could hope to know from philosophy. That is precisely why Jesus revealed the Father to us. If we could learn all we need to know about God from philosophy, we would have no need of divine revelation. Having said this, what philosophy has given us is not without worth. It shows that, at every moment of our existence, we depend on our Creator for everything: our existence, our intelligence, the intelligibilities our intelligence grasps, the goods we strive for—even the free choices by which we strive for them.

Is God a "He"?

One of the hottest controversies today about God concerns the traditional exclusive use of the pronoun *he.* Nearly all Christians admit that (1) God is not literally male, since he has no biological body, and (2) women are not essentially inferior to men. Those are red herrings.

There are, however, two reasons for defending the exclusive use of masculine pronouns and imagery for God. One issue is whether we have the authority to change the names of God used by Christ, the Bible and the Church. The traditional defense of masculine imagery for God rests on the premise that the Bible is divine revelation, not culturally relative, negotiable and changeable. As C. S. Lewis put it, "Christians believe God himself has told us how to speak of him."

The other reason for calling God "he" is historical. Except for Judaism, all other known ancient religions had goddesses as well as gods. The Jewish revelation was distinctive in its exclusively masculine pronoun because it was distinctive in its theology of the divine transcendence. That seems to be the main point of the masculine imagery. As a man comes into a woman from without to make her pregnant, so God creates the universe from without and impregnates our souls with grace or supernatural life from without. As a woman cannot impregnate herself, so the universe cannot create itself, nor can the soul redeem itself.

Surely there is an inherent connection between these two radically distinctive features of the three biblical or Abrahamic religions (Judaism, Christianity and Islam): their unique view of a transcendent God creating nature out of nothing and their refusal to call God "she" despite the fact that Scripture ascribes to him feminine *attributes* like compassionate nursing (Is 49:15), motherly comfort (Is 66:13) and carrying an infant (Is 46:3). The masculine pronoun safeguards (1) the transcendence of God against the illusion that nature is born from God as a mother rather than created and (2) the grace of God against the illusion that we can somehow save ourselves—two illusions ubiquitous and inevitable in the history of religion.

5

Creation and Evolution

There is much to be said about the issue of creation and evolution. However, here we only summarize the answers to five essential questions: (1) Is creation possible? (2) What difference does creation make? (3) Is evolution possible? (4) What difference does evolution make? (5) Does evolution contradict creation?

Is Creation Possible?

When Jewish and Christian theologians first talked to Greek philosophers, the Greeks thought the biblical notion that God created the world *ex nihilo* ("out of nothing") was absurd and irrational, because it violated a law of nature that *ex nihilo nihil fit* ("out of nothing nothing comes"). The reply was (and is) that

1. It is indeed a law of nature, but the laws of nature cannot be expected to bind the transcendent Creator of nature.
2. The reason for this is that all of nature and all powers in nature are finite, but God is infinite; no finite power can pro-

duce the infinite change from nonbeing to being, but infinite power can.

3. The idea of God creating out of nothing is not irrational because it does not claim that anything ever popped into existence without an adequate cause. God did not pop into existence, and nature did have an adequate cause: God.

What Difference Does the Doctrine of Creation Make?

The doctrine of creation affects our concept of God. If God is the Creator, he must be (1) infinitely powerful; (2) immeasurably wise; (3) a great artist; and (4) totally generous, since the all-sufficient, perfect Being couldn't have created out of need.

It also makes a difference to our concept of nature. If nature is created by God, it is (1) intelligible (it is no accident that science arose in the theistic West, not the pantheistic East); (2) good (thus Christianity has always condemned all forms of Manichaeism and gnosticism as heresy); and (3) real (the East often sees nature as an unreal illusion projected by unenlightened consciousness).

Finally, the doctrine of creation affects our concept of ourselves. If we owe our very existence to God, then (1) we have no rights over against God. How could Hamlet have rights over against Shakespeare? (2) Our existence is meaningful if we are in a play, a divine design, deliberately created rather than blindly evolved. (3) And if we owe God our very existence, we owe him everything.

Is Evolution Possible?

If evolution were impossible, that impossibility would have to come either from the creature or from the Creator.

Scientists and philosophers do not all agree about whether evolution is possible, whether the nature of species makes evolution impossible or not. The jury is still out, though many people on both sides feel absolutely and totally convinced.

There is no impossibility on the side of the Creator. If God wanted to arrange for species to evolve from each other by natural means, he certainly could have created such a world.

So as far as either scientists or theologians know, evolution is possible. Whether it is actual, whether it actually happened, is undecided. The theory is indeed in scientific trouble. Perhaps it can be salvaged. That is for science to decide.

What Difference Does Evolution Make?

We must distinguish three meanings that *evolution* can have.

First, it can mean simply a theory about *what* happened—more complex species appeared on earth—and *when,* as shown by the fossil record. Second, it can mean a theory about *how* this happened: by "natural selection," "the survival of the fittest." Third, it can mean the *absence* of a divine design, as distinct from God *using* natural selection. This third sense is not scientific at all, but philosophical and theological. One can accept evolution in sense 1 but not 2, or 1 and 2 but not 3. There is certainly a contradiction between the Bible and evolution in sense 3. But evolution in sense 3 is not a scientific theory at all.

If we evolved simply by blind chance, not divine design, then our lives have no overarching meaning, no preset divine plan, no script. The only meaning, purpose or values that exist are the ones we invent for ourselves. These can never be right or wrong, justified or not justified by a higher standard than our own desires, which created them. Thus there is no real reason to prefer Christian ethics to Stalinist ethics, for instance, except one's own desires themselves. Desire becomes its own reason, its own justification.

There is no logical contradiction between the Bible's claim that "in the beginning God created the heavens and the earth" (Gen 1:1 NIV) and the claim that once the earth was here, species evolved by natural selection. Science is like the study of the inner ecology of a fishbowl; the Bible is like a letter from the person who set up the fishbowl. Far from being logically exclusive, the two ideas of creation and evolution easily include each other or suggest each other. On the one hand, the Bible does not say that God "created" *(barā')* each species by a separate act, but that he said, "*Let the earth bring forth* living creatures" (Gen 1:24). On the other hand, a theory of evolution that confines itself to empirical science does not claim to know whether or not there is a divine Designer behind these natural forces. But surely such an elegant and ordered design strongly suggests a cosmic Designer.

There is also no logical contradiction between the Bible's claim that the human soul (the "image of God") is "breathed" ("spirited") into us from God, and evolution's claim that our body evolved from lower forms. Genesis 2:7 even suggests just such a double origin.

Does Evolution Contradict Creation?

God created the universe at the beginning of time; the *universe* could not possibly have evolved, because there was nothing for it to have evolved from, and not even any time for it to have evolved in. But what about *life* evolving? God may have created organic life directly or he may have developed it from inorganic life by natural processes; nothing we know for sure in either theology or science, God or nature, makes us absolutely certain of either answer.

Now the human body is one form of organic life. If organic life-forms evolved by natural selection, the human body may have done so too. Or God may have created it directly. Certainly a God who creates a whole universe from nothing can perform miracles within that universe, including creating that comparatively little thing called a human body, if that is what he wished to do. Nothing we know about either nature or God seems to make it impossible for our bodies either to have evolved or to have been created directly.

The soul, however, cannot evolve. Spirit cannot evolve from matter; it would be easier to get blood from a stone. No matter how many atoms you line up, or how complicated their lineup, you cannot get a wholly different thing—thought, consciousness, reason, self-awareness—from mere bits of matter. *Awareness of the material universe is not one more part of that universe.* The knowledge of a thing is not one of the thing's parts. It is transcendent to the thing, an addition from without.

6

Miracles

We begin with a preliminary definition. A miracle is *a striking and religiously significant intervention of God in the system of natural causes.*

Note two things here: (1) the concept of miracles presupposes, rather than sets aside, the idea that nature is a self-contained system of natural causes. Unless there are regularities, there can be no exceptions to them. (2) A miracle is not a contradiction. A man walking through a wall is a miracle. A man both walking and not walking through a wall at the same time and in the same respect is a contradiction. God can perform miracles but not contradictions—not because his power is limited but because contradictions are meaningless.

Two Questions About Miracles

We must distinguish the philosophical question—Are miracles possible?—from the historical question—Are miracles actual? Has there ever really been such an intervention? The answer to the second question requires a knowledge of events in history. It also requires not philosophical but historical investigation. What the philosopher and apologist can do is argue for the *possibility* of miracles. For nearly all those people who deny that miracles have actually happened have done so because of some philosophical argument which is supposed to prove that miracles *cannot* happen.

Obviously, you cannot believe miracles have happened without believing that a miracle-worker exists. Thus all who believe in miracles believe in some kind of God. But not everyone who believes in God believes in miracles. If there is a God, miracles are *possible.* But perhaps God did not choose to actualize this possibility.

There are two arguments for the possibility of miracles: one from the side of God, the miracle-worker, or the cause, and the other from the side of the world, or the effect. We must show that both God and the world are open, not closed, to miracles.

First, there is no defense against miracles in God's nature, no assurance that God would *not* work a miracle. For if there is a God, he is omnipotent (cf. chapter four) and thus able to work miracles. Whether he would freely choose to do so or not is not a matter we can know a priori, for it would depend on his free choice. An omnipotent God could not be compelled to work or not work a miracle. So there is no obstacle to miracles in God. If there is a God, miracles are possible.

Second, there is no obstacle to or defense against miracles on the part of the world of nature. If God created it in the first place, that is, if nature is open to the possibilities of existing or not existing, then it is open to the possibilities of containing miracles or not containing them. In other words, if God can bang out the Big Bang of creation, he can certainly add some smaller bangs of miracles. If the author can create the play, he can change it too.

Objections Against Miracles

The main task of the apologist, with regard to miracles, is to answer all the objections that seek to prove that miracles are impossible. Remember, the objector here is not a historian who has investigated every event in all of human history and concluded that not one of them is miraculous. We do not have to meet the objection on the historical level by showing that some particular events have been miraculous. Rather, the objections operate on the philosophical level, the level of possibility. Each objection tries to prove that miracles are impossible (or overwhelmingly improbable). If miracles are impossible, then they are not actual, and if no miracles ever actually happened, then Christianity is false. For the fundamental claims and doctrines of Christianity are all miracles: incarnation, resurrection, salvation, inspiration. If any one of these objections is valid, the whole of Christianity is refuted.

OBJECTION 1: *Miracles violate the principle of the uniformity of nature.*

Reply: What is meant by the "uniformity of nature"? If it means that we can explain whatever happens wholly in terms of the system of natural causes, then the objection begs the question. It amounts to saying "miracles violate the principle that miracles never happen."

OBJECTION 2: *A miracle, by definition, must violate some law of nature, and therefore must be a maximally improbable event. But then it is always more likely that the event never really occurred as described (or remembered), or that it did not really violate the laws of nature.*

Reply A: A miracle does not "violate" the laws of nature—any more than a school principal violates the schedule of classes by cancelling gym for a special assembly. *Violations* take place whenever someone who has to follow or uphold an established order fails or refuses to do so.

The Creator of the universe has authority over all creation. It is truly odd to call his suspending this or that regularly observed sequence a "violation," as if it were something he should feel guilty or embarrassed about. A miracle violates nothing. When one happens, God has (mercifully) modified the schedule of the day.

Reply B: Why are miracles called "maximally improbable"? They are certainly unusual, but how do we know whether they are *likely* to happen or not? Only if we have already decided whether or not it is likely that God exists—or that he would ever work a miracle.

OBJECTION 3: *How can we ever know that it is God and not a mere god (or even demon) who is responsible for this or that striking intervention in the natural order of things?*

Reply: Here again, context is crucial. When we consider, for example, the extraordinary deeds attributed to Jesus and the special relationship he claimed to have with "the Father" (i.e., God), it is difficult to avoid one of three conclusions. Either Jesus was a sincere lunatic, or a demonic fraud, or he really was the Son of God—and his extraordinary deeds were in the fullest sense miracles. This triple possibility arises not merely from the deeds considered by themselves; it arises primarily from the life, character and message of the one who performed them.

7

The Problem of Evil

There seems to be a logical contradiction built in to affirming all four of the following propositions:

1. God exists.

2. God is all-good.

3. God is all-powerful.

4. Evil exists.

Affirm any three and you must deny the fourth, it seems.

If God exists, wills only good, and is powerful enough to get everything he wills, then there would be no evil.

If God exists and wills only good, but evil exists, then God does not get what he wills. Thus he is not all-powerful.

If God exists and is all-powerful and evil exists too, then God wills evil to exist. Thus he is not all-good.

Finally, if "God" means "a being who is both all-good and all-powerful," and nevertheless evil exists, then such a God does not exist.

Five Possible Solutions

1. *Atheism* is the denial of proposition 1, that God exists.

2. *Pantheism* is the denial of proposition 2, that God is good and not evil.
3. Modern *naturalism* and ancient polytheism both deny proposition 3, that God is all-powerful. Ancient polytheism limited God's power by splitting God up into many little gods, some good, some evil. Modern naturalism, such as "process theology," does the same thing by reducing God to a being of time and growth and imperfection and weakness.
4. *Idealism* here means the denial of real evil. It comes in various forms, such as Advaita Hinduism, Christian Science and much New Age thinking, all of which say evil is an illusion of unenlightened human consciousness.
5. Finally, traditional *theism* (orthodox Christianity, Judaism and Islam) affirms all four propositions and denies they are logically contradictory. This can be done if and only if there are some ambiguous terms.

Defining *Evil*

The two most common misunderstandings about evil that make the problem more difficult than it needs to be are (1) the tendency to see evil as a being and (2) the confusion between two very different kinds of evil: physical evil and moral evil.

If evil were a being, the problem of evil would be insoluble, for then either God made it—and thus he is not all-good—or else God did not make it—and thus he is not the all-powerful creator of all things. But evil is not a *thing*. Things are not evil in themselves. For instance, a sword is not evil. Even the stroke of the sword that chops off your head is not evil in its being—in fact, unless it is a "good" stroke, it will not chop off your head. Where is the evil? It is in the will, the choice, the intent, the movement of the soul, which puts a wrong *order* into the physical world of things and acts—the order between the sword and an innocent's neck rather than a murderer's neck or an innocent's bonds.

Evil is real, but it is not a real *thing*. It is not subjective, but it is not an entity. Augustine defines evil as disordered love, disordered will. It is a wrong relationship, a nonconformity between our will and God's will. God did not make it; we did. That is the obvious point of Genesis 1 and 3, the stories of God's good creation and humanity's evil fall.

The second major misunderstanding about evil is to fail to distinguish between moral evil and physical evil, sin and suffering, the evil we actively do and the evil we passively suffer, the evil we freely will and the evil that is against our will, the evil we *are* directly responsible for and the evil we are not.

We need two different explanations for these two different kinds of evil, to explain both their causes and their cures. The origin of sin is human free will. The immediate origin of suffering is nature, or rather the relationship between ourselves and nature. We stub our toe, or get pneumonia, or drown.

Thus God is off the hook for sin, but not for suffering, it seems—unless the origin of suffering can also be traced to sin. This is what the story in Genesis 3 does. Without explaining how, it tells us that the thorns and thistles and the sweat of the brow and the pain of childbirth all are the result of our sin.

Connecting Suffering with Sin: The Fall

Connecting sin and suffering is not as fanciful as most people think, if we remember the principle of psychosomatic unity. This principle, affirmed by just about every one of the hundreds of schools of psychology, affirms that we are not ghosts in machines, souls imprisoned in bodies or angels in disguise, but soul-body ("psycho-somatic") unities. Our souls or psyches or personalities are our form and our bodies are our matter, much as in a poem the meaning is the form and the sounds or syllables are the matter.

Once we grant this principle, it makes sense that if the soul becomes alienated from God by sin, the body will become alienated too and experience pain and death as sin's inevitable consequences. These are not external, arbitrary punishments added on. Spiritual death (sin) and physical death go together because our spirits (souls, consciousness) and bodies go together.

According to the traditional interpretation, which we espouse here, the crucial question is whether the Fall actually happened in human history, not how literally you interpret the garden, the snake, the trees or the fruit. For if the modernist is right and Genesis 3 is not historical but only a fable that teaches that each of us sins, and that Adam and Eve are only symbols for Joe and Mary, then we have two terrible consequences.

First, if there never was a real time of innocence, then God did not make us good, as Genesis 1 says he did. If from the beginning we were sinners, then we can trace sin back to our beginning; and "in the beginning, God." Thus God is to blame for creating sinners.

Second, if the Fall is only what each one of us does, why have none of us ever resisted the forbidden fruit? If out of ten billion people, ten billion choose A and no one chooses B, we can hardly believe we have real freedom to choose between A and B. If the drama in Eden is only the drama of today in symbol, why isn't it dramatic today, why isn't it "iffy," why doesn't anyone ever choose Eden and innocence?

There are two powerful arguments for the historical truth of Genesis 3. First, nearly every tribe, nation and religion throughout history has a similar story. One of the most widespread "myths" (sacred stories) in the world is the myth of a past paradise lost, a time without evil, suffering or death. The mere fact that everyone innately believes the same thing does not prove that it is true, of course; but it is at least significant evidence. And if we assume what Chesterton calls "the democracy of the dead" and extend the vote to everyone, not just to "the small and arrogant oligarchy of the living," the few lucky ones who happen to be walking about in the strangest, most secularized society in history, it puts the onus of proof on the small modern minority who scorn the universal myth.

A second piece of experiential evidence for a historical time of innocence and a historical Fall are the four most salient facts about the human condition:

1. All desire perfect happiness.
2. No one is perfectly happy.
3. All desire complete certainty and perfect wisdom.
4. No one is completely certain or perfectly wise.

The two things we all want are the two things no one has. We behave as if we remember Eden and can't recapture it, like kings and queens dressed in rags who are wandering the world in search of their thrones. If we had never reigned, why would we seek a throne? If we had always been beggars, why would we be discontent? People born beggars in a society of beggars accept themselves as they are. The fact that we gloriously and irrationally disobey the first and greatest commandment of our modern prophets (the pop psychologists)—that we do *not* accept ourselves as we are—strongly points to the conclusion that we must at least unconsciously desire, and thus somehow remember, a better state.

To help understand creation and the Fall, the image of three iron rings suspended from a magnet is helpful. The magnet symbolizes God; the first ring, the soul; the middle ring, the body; and the bottom ring, nature. As long as the soul stays in touch with God, the magnetic life keeps flowing through the whole chain, from divine life to soul life, body life and nature life. The three rings stay harmonized, united, magnetized. But when the soul freely declares its independence from God, when the first iron ring separates from the magnet, the inevitable consequence is that the whole chain of rings is demagnetized and falls apart.

When the soul is separated from God, the body is separated from the soul—that is, it dies—and also from nature—that is, it suffers. For the soul's authority over the body is a delegated authority, as is humanity's authority over nature. When God the delegator is rejected, so is the authority he delegated. If you rebel against the king, his ministers will no longer serve you. Thus both suffering and sin are traced to man, not God.

Defining "Free Will"

Perhaps the clearest way to define our second crucial term, "free will," is to contrast it with the philosophy that denies it, that is, determinism.

According to determinism, everything we do can be totally accounted for by two causes: heredity plus environment. Free will adds a third cause to our actions: our wills, which in turn are not entirely the result of heredity.

Heredity and environment *condition* our acts, but they do not *determine* them, as the paints and the frame condition a painting but do not determine it. They are *necessary* causes but not *sufficient* causes of freely chosen acts.

The simplest argument for the existence of free will is observation of how we use words. We praise, blame, command, counsel, exhort and moralize to each other. Doing these things to robots is absurd. We do not hold machines morally responsible for what they do, no matter how complicated the machines are. If there is no free will, all moral meaning disappears from language—and from life.

The next question is, Why did God give us free will and allow us to misuse it? The question is misleading. One gives a polish to a table, or a pony to a child, but one does not give three sides to a triangle or free will to a human being. Free will is part of our essence. There can be no human being without it. The alternative to free will is not being a human but an animal or a machine.

Defining *Omnipotence*

A third term in need of definition is the term *omnipotence,* for the problem of evil is the apparent incompatibility of evil with a God who is all-powerful as well as all-good. If "all things are possible with God," why didn't God create a world without sin?

The answer is that he *did,* according to Genesis 1 and 2. Evil's source is not God's power but man's freedom. Then why didn't God create a world without human freedom? Because that would have been a world without humans, a world without hate but also without love. Love too proceeds only from free will. Animals cannot love, they can only like, or be affectionate.

But isn't a world with free human beings but no sin possible? It is indeed. And God created just such a world. But such a world—a world in which no-sin is freely possible—is necessarily a world in which sin is also freely possible. And if there are human beings at all, that is, creatures with free will, then it is up to their free choice whether that possibility of sin is freely actualized or not.

To put it another way, even omnipotence could not have created a world in which there was genuine human freedom and yet no possibility of sin, for our freedom includes the possibility of sin within its own meaning. "All things are possible with God" indeed; but a meaningless self-contradiction is not anything at all. One such meaningless self-contradiction is a world in which there is real free choice—that is, the possibility of freely choosing good or evil—and at the same time no possibility of choosing evil. To ask why God didn't create such a world is like asking why God didn't create colorless color or round squares.

Not all Christian thinkers agree with this concept of omnipotence. Some argue that God's power is limited by nothing, not even the laws of our logic. This view seems motivated by piety and the desire to credit God with every possible perfection. But a pious motive does not excuse a mental confusion. We believe this is a misunderstanding both of God and logic.

It is a misunderstanding of God in that it is not a divine perfection to create or perform a meaningless self-contradiction. It is rather God's consistency—his never contradicting himself—that is a perfection. There is also a misunderstanding here of what logic means. The law of noncontradiction is not "our" logic. It is not an artificial rule, like playing nine and not ten innings in baseball. It is an objective truth about everything. We discover it; we do not invent it. Nor is it a mere tautology, a verbal repetition like X = X. It is a universal, eternal, objective truth about all reality. It is based on the nature of God as one and identical and consistent with himself. To relativize or subjectivize or humanize the law of noncontradiction is to demean a divine attribute. *That* is impious.

Thus, even an omnipotent God cannot forcibly prevent sin without removing our freedom. This "cannot" does not mean that his power meets some obstacle outside himself, but rather (as Lewis said) that "nonsense does not cease to be nonsense when we add the words 'God can' before it."

Defining *Goodness*

First, we must be clear that *goodness* means more than "kindness." *Kindness* is the will to free the loved one from pain. Sometimes, to be good is *not* to be kind. Dentists, surgeons, athletic trainers, teachers and parents all know that. If *goodness* meant only kindness, a God who tolerated pain in his creatures when he could abolish it would not be an all-good God. A Christ who healed only a few thousand people in a world where millions were hurting would not be all-good either.

But the more deeply we love, the more we go beyond mere kindness. We are merely kind to a stranger's children but are more demanding of our own. We are merely kind to animals; we kill them to prevent pain. (Hence most advocates of euthanasia believe humans to be merely clever, evolved animals.)

But we have higher hopes for humans: we hope not just for freedom from pain but also freedom from vice and ignorance and sin.

God allows suffering and deprives us of the lesser good of pleasure in order to help us toward the greater good of moral and spiritual education. Even the pagans knew that: the gods teach wisdom through suffering.

God let Job suffer not because he lacked love but precisely out of his love, to bring Job to the point of the beatific vision of God face to face (Job 42:5), which is humanity's supreme happiness. Job's suffering hollowed out a big space in him so that a big piece of God and joy could fill it. Job's experience is paradigmatic for all saintly suffering.

He allows only the evil that can work for a greater good for us. Not all that we do is good, but all that God does is good, including *not* miraculously interfering to deliver us from all evil. That would be like parents doing all their children's homework problems for them.

Defining *Happiness*

We now come to our next ambiguous term, *happiness.* As with omnipotence and goodness, the ambiguity is between the shallow, popular meaning and the deeper, more philosophical meaning. The shallow meaning creates the problem of evil; the deeper meaning solves it.

The shallow meaning of happiness (which is our modern meaning) is first of all subjective. Happiness in this sense is a feeling. If you feel happy, you are happy. Second, this happiness is only a present, temporary phenomenon. Feelings come and go, and so does the feeling of happiness. Third, this happiness is largely a matter of "hap," that is, chance or fortune. It is "good luck." It is not under our control. Finally, its source is external. It consists in things like winning the lottery or the Super Bowl, or bodily pleasures, or prestige, or health. It is money, sex and power, never poverty, chastity and obedience.

The older, deeper meaning of happiness is evident in the Greek word *eudaimonia.* This is, first of all, an objective state, not just a subjective feeling. It's not true that if only you feel happy, you are happy. A grown man sitting in the bathtub all day playing with his rubber ducky may be content, but he is not happy. A Nero gloating over the Christians he killed may be pleased, but he is not happy. Happiness is to the soul what health is to the body. You can feel healthy without being healthy, and you can feel happy without truly being happy. You can also be happy without feeling happy, as Job was, learning wisdom through suffering. Jesus' saying "Blessed [objectively happy] are those who mourn [feel subjectively unhappy]" (Mt 5:4) assumes such a distinction.

In the second place, true happiness is a permanent state, a matter of a lifetime, not a fleeting moment. It is also under our control, our choice. Its main causes are wisdom and virtue, both of which are good habits we create in ourselves by practice, not gifts of fortune passively received. Finally, happiness's source is internal, not external. It is a good soul, not a good bank account, that makes you happy.

Divine providence arranges our lives in light of true happiness as our end, because God is good and loving. This does not necessarily include happiness in the shallow sense. In fact, to be truly happy, we need to be deprived of much happiness in the shallow sense. For true happiness requires wisdom, and wisdom requires suffering. As Rabbi Abraham Heschel said so simply, "The man who has not suffered, what can he possibly know, anyway?"

Deep happiness is in the spirit, not the body or even the feelings. It is like an anchor that holds fast and calm on the bottom even while storms rage on the surface. God allows physical and emotional storms to strengthen the anchor's hold, fires to test and harden our mettle. Our souls must become bright, hard, sharp swords. That is our destiny and his design. We are not toys; we are swords. And that requires tempering in the fire. The sword of the self is designed to sing in the sun eternally, like the seraphim. If we could catch even a glimpse of this heavenly destiny, if we understood why we are destined to judge angels (1 Cor 6:3), we would not see a problem in the sufferings of Job. Teresa of Ávila said that the most miserable earthly life, seen from the perspective of heaven, looks like one night in an inconvenient hotel.

Providence and Freedom

Once we understand the five terms discussed above, we can better understand the relation between God's providence and human freedom.

God knows all things, and his knowledge is eternal. Therefore he must know what we are going to choose before we ever choose it. But then how can we choose anything freely? Being free seems to involve an alternative; I may choose the path of vice or virtue. But if it has been determined from eternity that I will choose one path rather than another, there is really nothing for me to genuinely choose. God, in creating me, seems also to have created all my choices. So my choices turn out not to be mine at all but really God's. Two terrifying conclusions seem to follow: (1) if God exists, human freedom is impossible; and (2) God is the author of sin. Such is the problem of providence and freedom.

Our reply will be brief. First, when we say that God's knowledge is eternal or that he knows from all eternity the choices you are going to make, we do not mean that he knows at a time in the distant past that you will do something in the future and that this knowledge *determines* you to do it. We mean instead that the kind of knowledge God has (like the kind of being he has) is not limited in any way by temporal constraints as our knowledge is. Time is the measure of moving, changing beings;

in other words, time is a creature every bit as much as these things are. God, the Creator, is beyond such measure. His being transcends time and all such temporal categories.

We naturally think of God's eternity as if it were a temporal extension stretching infinitely back into the past and forward into the future. That is because our language reflects the kind of being we have: finite, changing, timebound. We know that God's being cannot really be like that and therefore that his knowledge cannot really look forward or back. He sees in a single and eternal act of vision all our free choices as they really exist, embedded in their times and places and circumstances.

Second, if God created us to be free, our freedom is a created gift. That is to say, God's creating and conserving power must be present in all our free acts. There can be no human freedom that is absolute in the sense that it eliminates the need for God. If God is really the Creator, the source of the being of all things, he must also give being to our freedom. His power cannot be an impediment to our free acts, as it would be if he were just another, but supremely powerful, creature—like a cosmic hypnotist, making us do his bidding when we think we are acting on our own. Creatures can act on their own only with respect to other creatures; but never with respect to the Creator. Without God there would be no freedom for us to have. And there would be no "us" to have it.

A great deal of technical theology has been written about the problems of providence and freedom. We decline to enter those dark and still turbulent waters. But as Christians we offer this thought: if God really is intimately involved in giving being to our free choices, to all our actions, think what a terrible thing sin must be. God has committed himself to create and sustain those of us who use the gift of freedom to hurt others and to hate God himself. The power of those who drove the nails into his beloved Son's hands and feet came ultimately from him. If freedom has a terrible price, surely God pays more than his share.

Practical Application

More important than evil as an argument against the existence of God is evil as a broken relationship with God, a spiritual divorce. Therefore, more important than a logical answer to the problem of evil theoretically is a personal answer to the problem of evil practically. More important than an apologist is a Savior.

The theoretical problem produces in us ignorance and questioning. The practical problem produces in us sin and guilt. Christ came to solve the second problem, not the first. Christ was not a philosopher.

Guilt can be removed only by God, because guilt is the index of a broken covenant with God. Shame is only the index of a horizontal, human fear or fracture, but guilt is vertical, supernatural. A good psychologist can set you free from shame but not from guilt. He can even set you free from guilt feelings, but not from real guilt. He can give you anesthetics but cannot cure your disease. Psychology can make you feel good, but only religion—relationship with God—can make you be good.

That's why God sent his Son; no one but Jesus Christ could take away our sin and guilt. Faith in his atoning sacrifice is the only answer to the real problem of evil. Our only hope is not a good *answer* but "good news," the gospel.

The great theologian Karl Barth was asked in his old age what was the most profound idea he had ever had, in his many years of theologizing. He instantly replied, "Jesus loves me."

8

The Divinity of Christ

The problem of Jesus' identity emerges from the data. The data are the four Gospels, which inform us about the claims he made about himself and the claims others made about him. In all four Gospels the claim is shockingly strong.

Jesus called himself the "Son of God"—that is, of the same nature as God. A son is of the same nature, the same species, the same essence, as his father. Jesus called God his Father: "The Father and I are one" (Jn 10:30) and "Whoever has seen me has seen the Father" (Jn 14:9).

He also claimed to be sinless: "Which of you convicts me of sin?" (Jn 8:46). He claimed to forgive sins—all sins, against everyone. The Jews protested: "Who can forgive sins but God alone?" (Lk 5:21). The only one who has the right to forgive all sins is the only one who is offended in all sins, namely, God. I have a right to forgive you for your sins against me, but not for your sins against others.

Jesus claimed to save us from sin and death. He said, "I am the resurrection and the life. Those who believe in me, even though they die, will live" (Jn 11:25). He said he had come from heaven, not just earth, and that he would return again from heaven at the end of the world to judge everyone (Mt 25:31-46). Meanwhile, he gave us his flesh to eat and said that this would give us eternal life (Jn 6:51).

Jesus changed Simon's name to Peter (Jn 1:42). For a Jew, changing names was something only God could do, for your name was not just a human, arbitrary label, but your real identity, which was given to you by God alone. In the Old Testament, only God changed names—and destinies: Abram became Abraham, Sarai became Sarah, Jacob became Israel. An orthodox Jew who got his name legally changed was excommunicated.

Jesus kept pointing people to himself, saying, "Come to me" (Mt 11:28). Buddha said, "Look not to me; look to my *dharma* (doctrine)." Buddha also said, "Be ye lamps unto yourselves." Jesus said, "I am the light of the world" (Jn 8:12). Lao Tzu taught the way *(tao);* Jesus said, "I am the way" (Jn 14:6).

Buddha, Confucius, Muhammad and other religious founders fulfilled no prophecies, performed no miracles and did not rise from the dead. Jesus did.

Most clearly and shockingly of all, he invited crucifixion (or stoning) by saying: "Very truly, I tell you [i.e., I am not exaggerating or speaking symbolically here; take this in all its force], before Abraham was, I AM" (Jn 8:58). He spoke and claimed the sacred name that God revealed to Moses, the name God used to name himself (Ex 3:14). If he was not God, no one in history ever said anything more blasphemous than this; by Jewish law, no one ever deserved to be crucified more than Jesus.

The Importance of the Issue

The issue is crucially important for at least two reasons.

1. The divinity of Christ is the most distinctively Christian doc-

trine of all. A Christian is most essentially defined as one who believes this.

2. The doctrine works like a skeleton key, unlocking all the other doctrinal doors of Christianity. Christians believe each of their many doctrines not because they have reasoned their own way to them as conclusions of a theological inquiry or as results of some mystical experiences, but on the divine authority of the One who taught them, as recorded in the Bible and transmitted by the church.

If Christ was only human, he could have made mistakes. Thus, anyone who wants to dissent from any of Christ's unpopular teachings will want to deny his divinity. And there are bound to be things in his teachings that each of us finds offensive if we look at the totality of those teachings rather than confining ourselves to comfortable and familiar ones.

Christians ought to realize how difficult, how scandalous, how objectionable, how apparently unbelievable and absurd this doctrine is bound to appear to others. They ought to realize this for two reasons: for apologetic purposes to understand the state of mind of prospective converts, and for purposes of appreciating their own belief in all its astounding character—something that dulls with familiarity.

Our argument for the truth of this doctrine consists of two steps. The first step is preliminary and consists of six clues. These clues merely show the *possibility* of God becoming man. The second step attempts to demonstrate that this actually happened in Jesus.

Some Clues to the Possibility of the Doctrine

1. C. S. Lewis calls the incarnation "myth become fact." Scattered generously throughout the myths of the ancient world is the strange story of a god who came down from heaven. Some tell of a god who died and rose for the life of man (e.g.,

Odin, Osiris and Mesopotamian corn gods). Just as the Garden of Eden story and the flood story appear in many different cultures, something like the Jesus story does too.

For some strange reason, many people think that this fact—that there are many mythic parallels and foreshadowings of the Christian story—points to the *falsehood* of the Christian story. Actually, the more witnesses tell a similar story, the more likely it is to be *true.* The more foreshadowings we find for an event, the more likely it is that the event will happen.

2. There is an analogy in art to the possibility of the Incarnation, an answer to the objection that it is impossible and self-contradictory. Suppose an author inserted himself into his own novel or play or movie as one of his own characters. This character would have a double nature and would have "come down from heaven," so to speak—the heaven of the author's mind—yet he would be a completely human character interacting with the other characters in the story. Alfred Hitchcock frequently did this, inserting himself into his own movies as a character for a fleeting moment. If he can do it, why can't God?

3. Which brings us to the very simple and logical argument: how do you, the critic who says the Incarnation is impossible, know so much that you can tell God what he can or cannot do? The skeptic should be more skeptical of himself and less skeptical of God.

4. The same point can be put more positively. If a being exists worthy of the name "God," that being must be omnipotent, that is, able to do anything that is intrinsically possible, anything that is meaningful, anything that does not involve a self-contradiction (like a rock that is not a rock, or a rock too heavy for infinite power to lift). But the Incarnation, however miraculous, is not a self-contradiction. Therefore the Incarnation is possible.

5. It is possible not only from the side of the Creator but also from the side of the creature. A human being can be transformed, taken up into God somewhat as subhuman food is transformed into the human body, physical vibratons are transformed into spiritual music, form and color become art, natural affection becomes charity or ego-consciousness becomes mystical experience. This principle of transformation runs throughout the world. Evolution, if it really happened, is an example of it. One might almost view Jesus as the next step in evolution. (The difference, of course, is that evolution—if it happens—happens by nature, while the Incarnation happened by supernatural grace. The point here is that both are possible.)
6. Finally, the fact that it is possible for one person to have two opposite natures can be seen (as we saw above) in the most familiar of all things: yourself. You are one person, yet you both are and are not spatially measurable. The gap between our physical and spiritual natures, between a few million electrons zapping across the synapses of Einstein's brain and his discovery that $E = MC^2$, is hardly less startling than the gap between the two natures of Christ. (Note: this is *not* meant to imply that Christ's divinity and humanity are to be identified with his soul and body, or that they are related in just the same way as our soul and our body.)

Arguments for Christ's Divinity

We now move to stronger arguments: arguments for the actuality, not just the possibility, of Christ's divinity.

Christ's trustworthiness. Everyone who reads the Gospels agrees that Jesus was a good and wise man, a great and profound teacher. Most nonreligious people, and even many people of other religions, like Gandhi, see him as history's greatest moral teacher. He is, in short, eminently trustworthy.

But what a trustworthy teacher teaches can be trusted. If he is trustworthy, then we should trust him, especially about his own identity. If we do not trust him about that, then we cannot say he is trustworthy, that is, wise and good.

The impossibility of the alternative. What is the alternative to the conclusion that Jesus is God? What do unbelievers say to this argument? Jesus claimed to be God, and Jesus is believable, therefore Jesus is God. The conclusion follows from the premises. Which premise can be denied?

Concerning the first one—that Jesus claimed to be God—perhaps the New Testament texts lie. Perhaps traditional Christianity is a myth, a fairy tale, a fantasy. But this raises questions even more unanswerable than the question of how a man could be God. Here are five such questions.

1. If the Gospels lie, who invented the lie, and for what reason? Was it Jesus' apostles? What did they get out of the lie? Martyrdom—hardly an attractive temptation. A liar always has some selfish motive.

2. Why did thousands suffer torture and death for this lie if they knew it was a lie? What force sent Christians to the lions' den with hymns on their lips? What lie ever transformed the world like that?

3. If it was not a deliberate lie but a hallucination or a myth sincerely mistaken for a literal truth, then who were the naive fools who first believed it? There isn't another idea a Jew would be less likely to believe. Imagine this: the transcendent God who for millennia had strictly forbidden his chosen people to confuse him with a creature as the pagans did, this Creator-God became a creature, a man—a crucified criminal. Hardly a myth that arises naturally in the Jewish mind!

4. And if it was not the Jews but the Gentiles who started the myth, where did the myth come from in the New Testament? Of the twenty-seven books of the New Testament, twenty-five

were written by Jews.

5. Whether Jews or Gentiles started the myth, they could not have done so during the lifetime of those who knew the real Jesus, for it would have been publicly refuted by eyewitnesses who knew the facts.

Aquinas argues that if the incarnation did not really happen, then an even more unbelievable miracle happened: the conversion of the world by the biggest lie in history and the moral transformation of lives into unselfishness, detachment from worldly pleasures and radically new heights of holiness all by a mere myth.

Lord, liar or lunatic? The dilemma is as old as the earliest Christian apologists: *Aut deus aut homo malus,* "Either God or a bad man." That is the classic argument. Spelled out, it looks like this:

1. Jesus was either God (if he did not lie about who he was) or a bad man (if he did).
2. But Jesus was not a bad man.
3. Therefore Jesus was (is) God.

Few would challenge the second premise. But if the first premise is added, the conclusion necessarily follows. Therefore, non-Christians must challenge the first premise. What justifies this premise?

Common sense. Someone who claims to be God and is not, is not a good man but a bad man.

Merely a "good man" is one thing Jesus could not possibly be. By claiming to be God he eliminated that possibility. For a liar is not a good man, and one who lies about his essential identity is a liar, and a mere man who claims to be God lies about his essential identity.

It is attractive and comfortable to say that Jesus was neither a bad man nor God, but a good man. To say he was a bad man offends Christians, and to say he was God offends non-Christians. To say neither offends no one. Therefore non-Christians want to say neither.

But that position offends logic.

Either Jesus believed his own claim to be God or he did not. If he did, he was a lunatic. If he did not, he was a liar. Unless, of course, he was (is) God.

Why could he not be either a liar or a lunatic? Because of his character. There are two things everyone admits about Jesus' character: he was wise and he was good. A lunatic is the opposite of wise, and a liar is the opposite of good.

There are lunatics in asylums who sincerely believe they are God. The "divinity complex" is a recognized form of psychopathology. Its character traits are well known: egotism, narcissism, inflexibility, dullness, predictability, inability to understand and love others as they really are and creatively relate to others. In other words, this is the polar opposite of the personality of Jesus! More than any other man in history, Jesus had the three essential virtues every human being needs and wants: wisdom, love and creativity.

If, on the other hand, Jesus was a liar, then he had to have been the most clever, cunning, Machiavellian, blasphemously wicked, satanic deceiver the world has ever known, successfully seducing billions into giving up their eternal souls into his hands. If orthodox Christianity is a lie, it is by far the biggest and baddest lie ever told, and Jesus is the biggest and baddest liar. But in every way Jesus was morally impeccable. He had all the virtues, both soft and hard, tender and tough. Further, he died for his "lie." What would motivate a selfish, evil liar to do that?

Suppose it was not Jesus himself but his disciples who invented the "lie"? The same arguments apply to the disciples, or to whoever first invented the "lie."

1. They do not manifest the psychological traits of liars.
2. There was no motive; they all got out of it the same thing Jesus did: suffering and death. They proved their sincerity by their martyrdom.
3. They could not have believed it would be successful because they would have known how every Jew would be shocked and horrified at this blasphemy.

What if it was his disciples who were the lunatics or the sincerely deceived ones? Suppose his divinity was their own idea that they read back into him and wrote back into the texts of the Gospels? The same arguments apply to whoever "invented" Christianity, whether it was Jesus, his apostles, the early church.

1. The writers of the Gospels certainly were not lunatics. If they invented their Jesus, they invented the most compelling fictional character in history. No lunatic could have invented a single chapter of the Gospels, much less all of it.
2. Nor could lunacy have changed so many lives for the better for so many centuries. Consider the enormity of the lunacy of confusing a man with God, then consider the enormity of the change wrought in millions of lives by this "lunacy" (read, e.g., Augustine's *Confessions*), and you will see the size of the camel you have to swallow to avoid swallowing the gnat of faith.
3. What accounts for the deception of whoever was first "deceived"? It is as hard to account for the origin of the lunacy as to account for the origin and motivation of the "lie."

Motives for Unbelief

Why, then, are many not compelled?

1. Not for rational reasons. No reason has ever been brought forth against Christianity that has not been refuted (see chapter two). The vast majority of those who disbelieve in

Christ's divinity disbelieve for other reasons, not because they have confronted the arguments.

2. Often, the thing hated and rejected is not Christ but Christians. Chesterton said, "The only good argument against Christianity is Christians."
3. Often, it is fear of the Church and its teachings and authority that scares people away. The Church is a concrete, visible, present institution that makes demands on our intellect to believe and on our will to practice a whole way of life that conflicts with our natural inclinations. Exactly like Jesus, who did the very same thing. The Church doesn't wield a club, but it does wave a cross.
4. The reluctance is usually moral. To admit that Jesus is divine is to admit his absolute authority over your life, including your private life, including your sex life. Can a drug addict think clearly and objectively about moral truth when it comes to drugs? Why should a sex addict be different?

   We are all addicts to something—to selfishness, at least. That is the meaning of sin, the very disease Jesus came to cure. Of course the cancer is going to fear the surgeon. That is exactly what you would expect. That is not a reason to disbelieve the surgeon's claim to be the specialist. Just the opposite.

   The old self in us is no fool. It sees that Christ comes to kill it. It knows Christianity is not a harmless theory but something alive and dangerous.
5. Some people are afraid of the mysterious and uncontrollable. If God did such a strange thing as becoming a man, then reality vastly escapes the neat and comfortable little boxes that some of us like to stuff it into.
6. There may also be simple pride, refusal to loose control of the reins of our lives.

7. It is also not at all intellectually fashionable to believe in Christ as anything more than a human teacher.
8. Finally, Americans' deepest religion is often equality. The notion that Christ alone is God and that all religions are *not* equal offends our real religion of equality, which makes no demands on us to discriminate and choose one and to justify that choice (see chapter fourteen).

None of these eight causes of unbelief is a reason, only a motive; that is, they are subjective, not objective; psychological, not logical.

9

The Resurrection

Every sermon preached by every Christian in the New Testament centers on the resurrection. The *gospel* or "good news" means essentially the news of Christ's resurrection. The message that flashed across the ancient world, set hearts on fire, changed lives and turned the world upside down was not "love your neighbor." Every morally sane person already knew that; it was not news. The news was that a man who claimed to be the Son of God and the Savior of the world had risen from the dead.

A reasonable challenge to the skeptic is this: if it can be proved that Jesus really rose from the dead, will you believe in him? For if he really rose, that validates his claim to be divine and not merely human, for resurrection from death is beyond human power; and his divinity validates the truth of everything else he said, for God cannot lie.

The resurrection is of crucial practical importance because it completes our salvation. Jesus came to save us from sin and its consequence, death (Rom 6:23).

The resurrection also sharply distinguishes Jesus from all other religious founders. The bones of Abraham and Muhammad and Buddha and Confucius and Lao Tzu and Zoroaster are all still here on earth. Jesus' tomb is empty.

The existential consequences of the resurrection can be seen by comparing the disciples before and after. Before, they huddled behind locked doors in fear and confusion. After, they were transformed from scared rabbits into confident saints, world-changing missionaries and courageous martyrs.

The greatest importance of the resurrection is not in the past—"Christ rose"—but in the present—"Christ is risen." The angel at the tomb asked the women, "Why do you look for the living among the dead?" (Lk 24:5). The same question could be asked today of mere historians and scholars. If only we did not keep Christ mummified in a casket labeled "history" or "apologetics," he would set our lives and world afire as powerfully as he did two millennia ago. That is the existential import of the resurrection.

The Strategy of the Argument for the Resurrection: Five Possible Theories

We believe Christ's resurrection can be proved with at least as much certainty as any universally believed and well-documented event in ancient history. To prove this, we do not need to presuppose anything controversial (e.g., that miracles happen). But the skeptic must also not presuppose anything (e.g., that they do not). We do not need to presuppose that the New Testament is infallible or divinely inspired or even true. We do not need to presuppose that there really was an empty tomb or postresurrection appearances, as recorded. We need to presuppose only two things, both of which are hard data, empirical data, which no one denies: the existence of the New Testament texts as we have them and the existence (but not necessarily the truth) of the Christian religion as we find it today.

The question is this: which theory about what really happened in Jerusalem on that first Easter Sunday can account for the data?

There are five possible theories: Christianity, hallucination, myth, conspiracy and swoon (see figure 3).

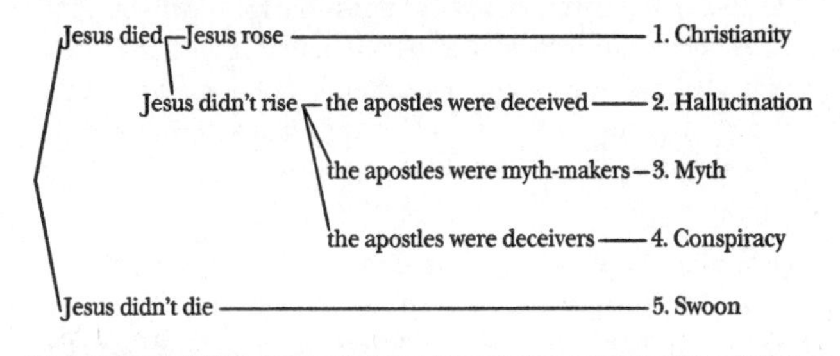

Figure 3

Refutation of the swoon theory: nine arguments. Is it possible that Jesus didn't actually die during the crucifixion but just fainted? Nine pieces of evidence refute the swoon theory:

1. Jesus could not have survived crucifixion. Roman procedures were very careful to eliminate that possibility. Roman law even laid the death penalty on any soldier who let a capital prisoner escape in any way, including bungling a crucifixion.
2. The fact that the Roman soldier did not break Jesus' legs, as he did to the other two crucified criminals (Jn 19:31-33), means that the soldier was sure Jesus was dead. Breaking the legs hastened the death so that the corpse could be taken down before the sabbath (Jn 19:31).
3. John, an eyewitness, certified that he saw blood and water come from Jesus' pierced side (Jn 19:34-35). This shows that Jesus' lungs had collapsed and he had died of asphyxiation. Any medical expert can vouch for this.
4. The body was totally encased in winding sheets and entombed (Jn 19:38-42).

5. The postresurrection appearances convinced the disciples, even "doubting Thomas," that Jesus was gloriously alive (Jn 20:19-29). It is psychologically impossible for the disciples to have been so transformed and confident if Jesus had merely struggled out of a swoon, badly in need of a doctor. A half-dead, staggering sick man who has just had a narrow escape is not worshiped fearlessly as divine Lord and conqueror of death.
6. How were the Roman guards at the tomb overpowered by a swooning corpse? Or by unarmed disciples? And if the disciples did it, they knowingly lied when they wrote the Gospels, and we are into the conspiracy theory, which we will refute shortly.
7. How could a swooning half-dead man have moved the great stone at the door of the tomb? Who moved the stone if not an angel? No one has ever answered that question.
8. If Jesus awoke from a swoon, where did he go? Think this through: you have a living body to deal with now, not a dead one. Why did it disappear? A man like that, with a past like that, would have left traces.
9. Most simply, the swoon theory necessarily turns into the conspiracy theory or the hallucination theory, for the disciples testified that Jesus did not swoon but really died and really rose.

Refutation of the conspiracy theory: seven arguments. Why couldn't the disciples have made up the whole story?

1. Pascal gives a simple, psychologically sound proof for why this is unthinkable:

> The hypothesis that the Apostles were knaves is quite absurd. Follow it out to the end, and imagine these twelve men meeting after Jesus' death and conspiring to say that he had risen from the dead. This means attack-

ing all the powers that be. The human heart is singularly susceptible to fickleness, to change, to promises, to bribery. One of them had only to deny his story under these inducements, or still more because of possible imprisonment, tortures and death, and they would all have been lost. Follow that out. (*Pensées* 322, 310)

2. If they made up the story, they were the most creative, clever, intelligent fantasists in history, far surpassing Shakespeare or Dante or Tolkien. Fishermen's "fish stories" are never that elaborate, that convincing, that life changing and that enduring.
3. The disciples' character argues strongly against such a conspiracy on the part of all of them, with no dissenters. They were simple, honest, common peasants, not cunning, conniving liars. They weren't even lawyers! Their sincerity is proved by their words and deeds. They preached a resurrected Christ and they lived a resurrected Christ. They willingly died for their "conspiracy." Nothing proves sincerity like martyrdom.
4. There could be no possible motive for such a lie. Lies are always told for some selfish advantage. What advantage did the "conspirators" derive from their "lie"? They were hated, scorned, persecuted, excommunicated, imprisoned, tortured, exiled, crucified, boiled alive, roasted, beheaded, disemboweled and fed to lions—hardly a catalog of perks!
5. If the resurrection were a lie, the Jews would have produced the corpse and nipped this feared superstition in the bud. All they had to do was go to the tomb and get it. The Roman soldiers and their leaders were on their side, not the Christians'. And if the Jews couldn't get the body because the disciples stole it, how did they do that? The arguments against the swoon theory hold here too: unarmed peasants

could not have overpowered Roman soldiers or rolled away a great stone while the guards slept on duty.

6. The disciples could not have gotten away with proclaiming the resurrection in Jerusalem—same time, same place, full of eyewitnesses—if it had been a lie. "If there had been a conspiracy, it would certainly have been unearthed by the disciples' adversaries, who had both the interest and the power to expose any fraud. Common experience shows that such intrigues are inevitably exposed" (Craig, *Knowing the Truth About the Resurrection,* chap. 6).

Refutation of the hallucination theory: thirteen arguments. If you thought you saw a dead man walking and talking, wouldn't you think it more likely that you were hallucinating than that you were seeing correctly? Why then not think the same thing about Christ's resurrection?

1. There were too many witnesses. Hallucinations are private, individual, subjective. Christ appeared to Mary Magdalene, to the disciples minus Thomas, to the disciples including Thomas, to the two disciples at Emmaus, to the fishermen on the shore, to James (his "brother" or cousin) and even to five hundred people at once (1 Cor 15:3-8). Even three different witnesses are enough for a kind of psychological trigonometry; over five hundred is about as public as you can wish. And Paul says in this passage (v. 6) that most of the five hundred are still alive, inviting any reader to check the truth of the story by questioning the eyewitnesses. He could never have done this and gotten away with it, given the power, resources and numbers of his enemies, if it were not true.
2. The witnesses were qualified. They were simple, honest, moral people who had firsthand knowledge of the facts.
3. The witnesses saw Christ together, at the same time and place.

4. Hallucinations usually last a few seconds or minutes; rarely hours. This one hung around for forty days (Acts 1:3).
5. Hallucinations usually happen only once, except to the insane. This one returned many times, to ordinary people (Jn 20:19—21:14; Acts 1:3).
6. Hallucinations come from within, from what we already know, at least unconsciously. This one said and did surprising and unexpected things (Acts 1:4, 9)—like a real person and unlike a dream.
7. Not only did the disciples not expect this, they didn't even believe it at first—neither Peter, nor the women, nor Thomas, nor the eleven. They thought he was a ghost; he had to eat something to prove he was not (Lk 24:36-43).
8. Hallucinations do not eat. The resurrected Christ did, on at least two occasions (Lk 24:42-43; Jn 21:1-14).
9. The disciples touched him (Mt 28:9; Lk 24:39; Jn 20:27).
10. They also spoke with him, and he spoke back. Figments of your imagination do not hold profound, extended conversations with you, unless you have the kind of mental disorder that isolates you. But this "hallucination" conversed with at least eleven people at once, for forty days (Acts 1:3).
11. The apostles could not have believed in the "hallucination" if Jesus' corpse had still been in the tomb. This is a very simple and telling point; for if it was a hallucination, where was the corpse? They would have checked for it; if it was there, they could not have believed.
12. If the apostles had hallucinated and then spread their hallucinogenic story, the Jews would have stopped it by producing the body—unless the disciples had stolen it, in which case we are back with the conspiracy theory and all its difficulties.

13. A hallucination would explain only the postresurrection appearances; it would not explain the empty tomb, the rolled-away stone or the inability to produce the corpse. No theory can explain all these data except a real resurrection.

Refutation of the myth theory: six arguments. How do we know Christ's resurrection isn't just a myth?

1. The style of the Gospels is radically and clearly different from the style of all the myths. Any literary scholar who knows and appreciates myths can verify this. There are no overblown, spectacular, childishly exaggerated events. Nothing is arbitrary. Everything fits in. Everything is meaningful. The hand of a master is at work here.

   Psychological depth is at a maximum. In myth it is at a minimum. In myth, such spectacular external events happen that it would be distracting to add much internal depth of character. That is why it is ordinary people like Alice who are the protagonists of extraordinary adventures like Wonderland. The character depth and development of everyone in the Gospels—especially, of course, Jesus himself—is remarkable.

   It is also done with an incredible economy of words. Myths are verbose; the Gospels are laconic.

   There are also telltale marks of eyewitness description, like the little detail of Jesus writing in the dirt when asked whether to stone the adulteress or not (Jn 8:6). No one knows why this is put in; nothing comes of it. The only explanation is that the writer saw it. If this detail and others like it throughout all four Gospels were invented, then a first-century tax collector (Matthew), a "young man" (Mark), a doctor (Luke) and a fisherman (John) all independently invented the new genre of realistic fantasy nineteen centuries before it was reinvented in the twentieth.

2. A second problem is that there was not enough time for

myth to develop. The original demythologizers pinned their case onto a late second-century date for the writing of the Gospels; several generations have to pass before the added mythological elements can be mistakenly believed to be facts.

Julius Muller challenged his nineteenth-century contemporaries to produce a single example anywhere in history of a great myth or legend arising around a historical figure and being generally believed within thirty years after that figure's death. No one has ever answered him.

3. The myth theory posits two layers. The first layer is the historical Jesus, who was not divine, did not claim divinity, performed no miracles and did not rise from the dead. The second, later, mythologized layer is the Gospels as we have them, with a Jesus who claimed to be divine, performed miracles and rose from the dead. The problem with this theory is simply that there is not the slightest bit of any real evidence whatever for the existence of any such first layer. The two-layer-cake theory has the first layer made entirely of air.

4. A little detail, seldom noticed, is significant in distinguishing the Gospels from myth: the first witnesses of the resurrection were women. In first-century Judaism, women had low social status and no legal right to serve as witnesses. If the empty tomb were an invented legend, its inventors surely would not have had it discovered by women, whose testimony was considered worthless. If, on the other hand, the writers were simply reporting what they saw, they would have to tell the truth, however socially and legally inconvenient.

5. The New Testament could not be myth misinterpreted and confused with fact because it specifically distinguishes the two and repudiates the mythic interpretation (2 Pet 1:16). Since it explicitly says it is not myth, if it *is* myth, it is a delib-

erate lie rather than myth. The dilemma still stands: it is either truth or lie, whether deliberate (conspiracy) or nondeliberate (hallucination). There is no escape from the horns of this dilemma. Once a child asks whether Santa Claus is real, your "yes" becomes a lie, not myth, if he is not literally real. Once the New Testament distinguishes myth from fact, it becomes a lie if the resurrection is not a fact. R. L. Purtill summarizes the textual case:

> Many events which are regarded as firmly established historically have (1) far less documentary evidence than many biblical events, (2) and the documents on which historians rely for much secular history are written much longer after the event than many records of biblical events. (3) Furthermore, we have many more copies of biblical narratives than of secular histories, and (4) the surviving copies are much earlier than those on which our evidence for secular history is based. If the biblical narratives did not contain accounts of miraculous events . . . biblical history would probably be regarded as much more firmly established than most of the history of, say, classical Greece and Rome. (*Thinking About Religion,* pp. 84-85)

If everything we have said so far is true, a surprising consequence necessarily follows: there are only two things that are needed for anyone to be converted to Christ. (Grace is also needed from God, of course, but God is willing to give his grace to anyone who is willing to seek and receive it.) These two things are awareness of the data and intellectual and moral honesty. This is exactly the attitude most unbelievers praise and claim to have: tough-minded, skeptical, scientific, logical honesty. Well, if they really have that, it will lead them to Christ.

10

The Bible: Myth or History?

The Bible, miracles and the resurrection are closely linked in modern apologetics. They typically stand or fall together. Most of those who do not believe that Christ physically rose from the dead disbelieve for two reasons: (1) "miracles like that don't really happen," and (2) "the Bible is myth, not history."

It is important at the outset to clarify the logical order and relationship among the three issues of the Bible, miracles and the resurrection, because those who argue against a literal resurrection and against miracles on the grounds that the Bible is myth, not history, are arguing backwards. The logic goes the other way: if the resurrection really did happen, then the assumption that "miracles don't happen" is refuted; in that case, the miracle stories in the Bible can be history, not myth.

Let us put the logical point in a different way. To argue that the resurrection didn't really happen because the Bible is myth begs the question. For when unbelievers are asked why they think the Bible is myth rather than history, they say it is because it is full of unbelievable miracle stories like the resurrection. This is arguing in a circle. It is arguing that the resurrection is myth because the Bible is myth, and the Bible is myth because it contains obviously mythical miracle stories like the resurrection.

The Role of Scripture in Apologetics

We want to avoid two extremes here: the fundamentalist extreme and the modernist extreme.

The fundamentalist extreme. Most fundamentalists, as well as many who call themselves not fundamentalists but evangelicals, will do apologetics only from the starting point of the authority of Scripture. We think this is a tactical error. There are three points to their tactics that seem questionable.

1. They think that it is *necessary* to begin by convincing you of the authority of Scripture because they think that natural human reason alone, apart from Scripture, is not strong enough or good enough to direct unbelievers to belief.
2. They think that therefore the only right order in apologetics is first to prove the authority of Scripture, and then to move on to other apologetic questions with this all-important weapon in hand.
3. They think that special standards must be used to understand and interpret Scripture since, unlike all other books, it is not just man's words about God but God's word about man.

But remember: for many years early Christian apologists and Church fathers argued quite effectively for Christianity without even *having* the New Testament Scriptures as authoritatively defined, since the canon was not established until generations later. And down through the centuries many people have in fact been led to belief—at least belief in a Creator God and in the *possibility* of salvation—through rational arguments not based on Scripture. (Of course, saving faith, as distinct from intellectual belief, is not the work of reason alone.)

Also, it is very difficult to prove the authority of Scripture *first* to the unbeliever. It is much easier to prove something like the existence of God (chapter three), or even the divinity of Christ (chapter eight), where arguments can be simple, short and clear in a way that the arguments for the authority of Scripture can never be. Traditional apologetics, Protestant as well as Catholic, has more often used the opposite order, coming to the authority of Scripture later. Instead of

1. Scripture is infallible;
2. therefore Christ is infallible;
3. therefore Christ is divine;

the more convincing order is

1. Scripture is *reliable* as historical record, as data;
2. Christ's claims to divinity are found in Scripture;
3. then comes the argument for the truth of these claims (chapter eight).

You don't need to prove scriptural infallibility first to confront someone with the claims of Christ.

The third difficulty is that the unbeliever will not accept the use of any special standards or assumptions or attitudes toward Scripture at the outset, since they clearly beg the question. You must first prove that Scripture *deserves* such special treatment as the Word of God, and you must prove this without presupposing it, without giving Scripture special treatment. Otherwise you argue in a circle, assuming what you need to prove.

The modernist extreme. Modernists make the opposite mistake from fundamentalists about Scripture. If fundamentalists worship it, modernists trash it. But strangely, the two extremes share a common mistake. Both sides use special standards to judge the Bible, standards that are not used to judge other books.

Fundamentalists interpret everything, or everything they possibly can, literally and insist right from the start on a believing attitude toward the Bible. Modernists interpret everything, or at least everything miraculous or supernatural (or morally unpopular), nonliterally and insist right from the start on an unbelieving, skeptical attitude toward the Bible.

Typical modernist Scripture scholarship is *not* objective or neutral historical and textual scholarship. It is *eisegesis* ("reading into") rather than *exegesis* ("reading out of"); it reads a particular modern worldview—naturalism, denial of the supernatural and miracles—into the texts and judges the texts on the basis of that worldview. Indeed, modernists commit a graver version of the very error they accuse fundamentalists of, for fundamentalists only read into the text the same worldview it contains—supernaturalism—while modernists impose an alien and modern worldview on it. Fundamentalists do not add miracles to the textual data; modernists subtract them. This is fudging the data to conform to the theory—the fundamental fallacy of bad science. It is the modernist who is being unscientific here.

Unbelievers say (1) that Christianity is what the New Testament teaches and (2) that Christianity is false. Christians say (1) that Christianity is what the New Testament teaches and (2) that Christianity is true. Modernist theologians want to make peace with both sides, so they say (1) that Christianity is *not* what the New Testament, at face value, teaches but instead is what modernists have selected out of the New Testament (the love ethic without the miracles) as something that will be acceptable to both unbelievers and believers and (2) that this redefined Christianity is true.

But will Scripture allow Christianity to be redefined? See Galatians 1:8 for an answer.

The whole point of the Bible, "the Word of God" on paper, is to reveal and lead us to Christ, "the Word of God" in human flesh. In the chapter on Christ's divinity, our argument assumed the historical data of the Gospels. We must now argue for our data. For in our argument for Christ's divinity, all three hypotheses—Lord, liar and lunatic—assumed that Jesus *claimed* divinity. Suppose he didn't. Suppose this claim is a myth (in the sense of fiction). Suppose the liar is not Jesus but the New Testament texts.

This supposition is by far the most widespread intellectual reason why Christians in the twentieth century have lost their faith. For each one who thinks that the problem of evil or the progress of science has refuted religion, there are ten who think that textual scholarship, the "historical-critical method" and "higher criticism" have done so by reducing the New Testament texts to myth. Not atheistic philosophers or skeptical scientists but biblical theologians have performed the miracle of changing wine to water, faith to myth.

The data itself makes the myth hypothesis impossible. Here's how:

1. If the same neutral, objective, scientific approach is used on the New Testament texts as is used on all other ancient documents, then the texts prove remarkably reliable. Complex, clever hypothesis after hypothesis follow one another with bewildering rapidity and complexity in the desperate attempt to debunk, "demythologize" or demean the data—like declawing a lion. No book in history has been so attacked, cut up, reconstituted and stood on its head as the New Testament. Yet it still lives—like Christ himself.

2. The state of the manuscripts is very good. Compared with any and all other ancient documents, the New Testament stands up as ten times more sure. For instance, we have five hundred different copies earlier than A.D. 500. The next most reliable ancient text we have is the *Iliad*, for which we have only fifty copies that date from five hundred years or less after its origin.

We have only one very late manuscript of Tacitus's *Annals*, but no one is reluctant to treat that as authentic history. If the books of the New Testament did not contain accounts of miracles or make radical, uncomfortable claims on our lives, they would be accepted by every scholar in the world. In other words, it is not objective, neutral science but subjective prejudice or ideology that fuels skeptical Scripture scholarship.

The manuscripts that we have, in addition to being old, are also mutually reinforcing and consistent. There are very few discrepancies and no really important ones. And all later discoveries of manuscripts, such as the Dead Sea Scrolls, have confirmed rather than refuted previously existing manuscripts in every important case. There is simply no other ancient text in nearly as good a shape.

3. If Jesus' divinity is a myth invented by later generations ("the early Christian community," often code for "the inventors of the myth"), then there must have been at least two or three generations between the original eyewitnesses of the historical Jesus and the universal belief in the new, mythic, divinized Jesus; otherwise, the myth could never have been believed as fact because it would have been refuted by eyewitnesses of the real Jesus. Both disciples and enemies would have had reasons to oppose this new myth.

However, we find no evidence at all of anyone ever opposing the so-called myth of the divine Jesus in the name of an earlier merely human Jesus. The early "demythologizers" explicitly claimed that the New Testament texts had to have been written after A.D. 150 for the myth to have taken hold. But no competent scholar today denies the first-century dating of virtually all of the New Testament—certainly Paul's letters, which clearly affirm and presuppose Jesus' divinity and the fact that this doctrine was already universal Christian orthodoxy.

4. If a mythic "layer" had been added later onto an originally merely human Jesus, we should find *some* evidence, at least indirectly and secondhand, of this earlier layer. We find instead an absolute and total absence of any such evidence anywhere, either internal (in the New Testament texts themselves) or external, anywhere else, in Christian, anti-Christian or non-Christian sources.

5. The style of the Gospels is not the style of myth but that of real, though unscientific, eyewitness description. Anyone sensitive to literary styles can compare the Gospels to any of the mythic religious literature of the time, and the differences will appear remarkable and unmistakable: for instance, the intertestamental apocalyptic literature of both Jews and Gentiles, or pagan mythic fantasies like Ovid's *Metamorphoses* or Flavius Philostratus's story of the wonder-worker Apollonius of Tyana (A.D. 220).

   If the events recorded in the Gospels did not really happen, then these authors invented modern realistic fantasy nineteen centuries ago. The Gospels are full of little details that are found only in eyewitness descriptions or modern realistic fiction. They also include dozens of details of life in first-century Israel that could not have been known by someone not living in that time and place (see Jn 12:3, for instance). And there are *no* second-century anachronisms, either in language or content.

6. The claim of Jesus to be God makes sense of his trial and crucifixion. The Jewish sensitivity to blasphemy was unique; no one else would so fanatically insist on death as punishment for claiming divinity. Throughout the Roman world, the prevailing attitude toward the gods was "the more, the merrier."

   Jesus' politics cannot explain his crucifixion. He had no political ambitions. The main reason why most Jews rejected his claim to be the Messiah was that he did *not* liberate them from Roman political oppression.

Why then was he crucified? The political excuse that he was Caesar's rival was a lie trumped up to justify his execution, since Roman law did not recognize blasphemy as grounds for execution and the Jews had no legal power to enforce their own religious laws of capital punishment under Roman rule.

7. There are four Gospels, not just one. Matthew, Mark, Luke and John were written by four different writers, at four different times, probably for four different audiences and with four somewhat different purposes and emphases. So a lot of cross-checking is possible. By a textual trigonometry or triangulation, we can fix the facts with far greater assurance here than with any other ancient personage or series of events. The only inconsistencies are in chronology (only Luke's Gospel claims to be in exact order) and accidentals like numbers (e.g., did the women see one angel or two at the empty tomb?).

8. If the divine Jesus of the Gospels is a myth, who invented it? Whether it was his first disciples or some later generation, no possible motive can account for this invention. For until the Edict of Milan in A.D. 313, Christians were subject to persecution, often tortured and martyred, and hated and oppressed for their beliefs. No one invents an elaborate practical joke in order to be crucified, stoned or beheaded.

9. First-century Jews and Christians were not prone to believe myths. They were already more "demythologized" than any other people. The orthodox were adamantly, even cantankerously and intolerantly, opposed to the polytheistic myths of paganism and to any ecumenical syncretism. Nor would anyone be less likely to confuse myth and fact than a Jew. Peter explicitly makes the point that the Gospel story is his-

torical fact, not "cleverly devised myths" (2 Pet 1:16).

10. Finally, if you read the Gospels with an open mind and heart, you may well conclude, along with Dostoyevsky and Kierkegaard, that no mere man could possibly have invented this story.

11

Life After Death

The human race has come up with six basic theories about what happens to us when we die:

1. *Materialism:* Nothing survives; death ends all of me. Seldom held before the eighteenth century, materialism is now a strong minority view in industrialized nations. It is the natural accompaniment of atheism.
2. *Paganism:* A vague, shadowy semi-self or ghost survives and goes to the place of the dead, the dark, gloomy Underworld.
3. *Reincarnation:* The individual soul survives and is reincarnated into another body.
4. *Pantheism:* Death changes nothing, for what survives death is the same as what was real before death: only the one, changeless, eternal, perfect, spiritual, divine, all-inclusive Reality, sometimes called by a name ("Brahman") and sometimes not (as in Buddhism).
5. *Immortality of the soul:* The individual soul survives death, but not the body.

6. *Resurrection:* At death, the soul separates from the body and is reunited at the end of the world to its new, immortal, resurrected body by a divine miracle. This is the Christian view. This view, the supernatural resurrection of the body rather than the natural immortality of the soul alone, is the only version of life after death in Scripture. It is dimly prophesied and hoped for in the Old Testament, but clearly revealed in the New.

For both 5 and 6, the individual soul survives bodily death. That is the point we shall prove here.

The Argument from the Soul's Simplicity

Major premise: What is not composed cannot be decomposed. Whatever is composed of parts can be decomposed into its parts: a molecule into atoms, a cell into molecules, an organ into cells, a body into organs, a person into body and soul. What is not composed of parts cannot be taken apart.

Minor premise: The soul is not composed of parts. It has no countable, quantifiable parts as the body does. You can cut a body in half but not a soul; you can't have half a soul. You don't cut an inch off your soul when you get a haircut.

Conclusion: Therefore the soul is not decomposable.

Now there are only two ways of being destroyed: by being decomposed into parts, as the body is, or by being annihilated as a whole. But we know of nothing that is ever annihilated as a whole. Nothing simply pops out of existence. If the soul dies neither in parts (by decomposition) nor as a whole (by annihilation), then the soul does not die.

The Argument from the Soul's Power to Objectify the Body

Major premise: If there is a power of the soul that cannot come from the body, this indicates that the soul is not a part or a function of the body. That, in turn, indicates that it is not subject to the laws of the body, including mortality.

Minor premise: Such a power of the soul exists which could not come from the body. It is the power to objectify the body. The body cannot objectify itself, be its own object of knowledge, or know itself. To objectify X, I must be more than X. I can know a stone as an object only because I am not merely a stone as object. The projecting machine can project images on the screen only because it is not merely one more image. I can remember my past only because I am more than my past; I am a present knower. (My present is alive; my past is dead.) I can know my body as object only because I am more than my body. The knowing subject must be more than the known object.

Conclusion: Therefore the soul is not subject to the body's mortality.

The Argument from Two Immaterial Operations

Major premise: If I perform operations in which the body plays no intrinsic or essential role, operations which are not operations of the body, then I am more than my body; I am also an immaterial soul (which need not die when the body dies).

Minor premise: Two such operations are (1) thinking, as distinct from external sensing or internal sensing (imagining), and (2) deliberate, rational, responsible willing, as distinct from instinctive liking, desiring or feeling.

Conclusion: I am an immaterial and immortal soul.

Proof of (1): We can know by introspection that our thought is not limited to images, like pyramids, but can also understand abstract, immaterial, universal essences and principles, like triangularity and trigonometry. We cannot imagine the difference between a 103-sided figure and a 104-sided figure as we can imagine the difference between a 3-sided figure and a 4-sided figure; but we can understand the difference between a 103-sided figure and a 104-sided figure, even though we cannot imagine it. Therefore our understanding transcends our imagining.

Proof of (2): If willing is only instinctive desiring, two absurd conclusions follow. (a) None of us would be free and in control of our willing, therefore none of us would be responsible for our choices, thus all praise and blame and responsibility would be illusion. (b) If there were only instinct in us and not will, then the strongest instinct would always win. But this is not the case, for I can and sometimes do choose contrary to my strongest instinct (e.g., when I choose to follow the weaker instinct of compassion rather than the stronger instinct of fear and self-preservation in going to the aid of a victim who is drowning or being mugged).

The Antimaterialist Self-Contradiction Argument

A computer is not reliable if it has been programmed by chance rather than by rational design (e.g., by hailstones falling at random on its keyboard).

The human brain and nervous system are a computer. They may be much more, but they are not less than a computer. So the human brain is not reliable if it has been programmed by mere chance.

But if materialism is true, if the soul is only the brain, if there is no spirit, no human soul and no God, then the brain has been programmed by mere chance. All the programming our brains have received, through heredity (genetics) and environment (society), is ultimately only unintelligent, undesigned, random chance, brute facts, physical causes, not logical reasons.

Therefore materialism cannot be true. It refutes itself. It destroys its own credentials. If the brain is nothing but blind atoms, we have no reason to trust it when it tells us about anything, including itself and atoms. Thus, if there is nothing but atoms, we have no reason to believe there is nothing but atoms.

If materialism is not true, this means there is immaterial reality too. And that immaterial reality—usually called spirit, or soul—need not be subject to the laws of material reality, including the law of mortality.

The Argument from Ultimate Justice

Since justice is often not done in the short run in human life on earth, either (1) justice *is* done in the long run—in which case there must be a "long run," a life after death—or else (2) this absolute demand we make for moral meaning and ultimate justice is not met by reality but is a mere subjective quirk of the human psyche—in which case there is no foundation in reality for our deepest moral instincts, no objective validity or justification for justice. The statement "I want justice" only tells something about us, like "I feel sick," not about objective reality, what really is or what really ought to be.

The argument does not prove life after death simply and absolutely, but it shows what price must be paid to deny it: the price of moral seriousness. Once we stop believing that morality has a basis in objective reality, once we start believing that morality is nothing more than subjective feelings and wishes, once we reduce justice from a cosmic law to a private preference, we no longer see it as binding or fear to disobey it when it is inconvenient. As Dostoyevsky notes, "If there is no immortality, everything is permitted."

Pascal's Wager

The Wager was for Pascal an argument for believing in God. It can also be used as an argument for believing in life after death.

For skeptically inclined people, arguments based on the fact that we do *not* know something—arguments from ignorance—are more convincing than arguments based on supposed knowledge, which the skeptic can question. For instance, the argument against abortion from the fact that you can't be sure that the fetus is not a human being is a stronger argument for such a skeptic than the argument from the premise that we know for sure that the fetus is a human being.

The "wager" argument does not prove that life after death exists, only that it is foolish not to believe in it.

If the Christian claim is true, the only chance for gaining eternal happiness is by believing. "Whoever does not believe will be condemned" (Mk 16:16 NIV). Perhaps that is false—but perhaps it is true. How foolish to ignore the second possibility. "For what does it profit a man to gain the whole world, and forfeit his soul?" (Mk 8:36, NASB).

The Argument from *Sehnsucht* (Longing)

Major premise: Every natural, innate desire in us—as distinct from artificial and conditioned desires—corresponds to a real object which can satisfy that desire. If there is hunger, there is food; if thirst, drink; if eros, sex; if curiosity, knowledge; if loneliness, society. It would be surpassing strange if we found creatures falling in love in a sexless world.

Minor premise: There exists in us one desire that nothing in this life can satisfy, a mysterious longing *(Sehnsucht)* that differs from all others in that its object is undefinable and unattainable in this life.

Although we do not clearly understand exactly what it is that we want, we all do in fact by our nature want paradise, heaven, eternity, the divine life. Augustine said, "Our hearts are restless until they find their rest in Thee"—even if we don't know who or what "Thee" is. Something deep in our souls is not satisfied with this whole world of time and mortality.

Conclusion: Therefore this "more"—eternal life—exists.

Complaint about anything shows that there must be an alternative, something more and better. We do not complain about being, or about 2 + 2 making 4. But we complain about pain and ignorance and poverty. We also complain about time; there is never enough of it—even now, and certainly when we are dying. We want more than time; we want eternity. Therefore there must be eternity. We complain about this world. It is never good enough. Therefore there must be another world that *is* good enough. We may not attain it, just as we may die of starvation. But the innate hunger for it proves that it exists, just as the innate hunger for food proves that food exists.

The Argument from Love

The argument from love, inspired by Gabriel Marcel, is less "tight" but deeper than most others; it depends more on a "seeing" than on strict logical compulsion. Yet it can be formulated logically as follows.

1. *Love* here means *agapē,* not *eros;* gift-love, not need-love; love of the other, not love of enjoyment.
2. This love is not blind. It has eyes. "The heart has its reasons." We all instinctively know this, for if we were asked who knows us best, someone less bright who loves us more or someone more bright who loves us less, we all know that the one who loves us best knows us best. *Eros* may be blind, but *agapē* is just the opposite of blind. How could love be blind if God is love? God is not blind!
3. What love sees is the intrinsic value of the beloved. If I do not love you, I see you as one of the many objects in my world—something replaceable, like a ballplayer or an actor. Your value there is your ability to perform certain functions, which others could also perform; therefore you are not indispensable. But the one thing no one else can ever do is to be you. I see your indispensability only if I love you for your own sake, not for my sake or for your function's sake.
4. On this basis, I can now argue that it is morally intolerable that the indispensable be dispensed with, the irreplaceable replaced.

5. Why couldn't this morally intolerable situation be real? Because if it were, then reality—ultimate, universal, cosmic reality—would do to all persons in the end what is morally intolerable, what we should never do; in that case our values would have no ground in reality.
6. Therefore, either moral values are groundless, or persons are not dispensed with but live forever. The eye of death seems to see the eclipse of love, but the eye of love sees the eclipse of death. Thus C. S. Lewis could write the following remarkable epitaph on the death of his friend Charles Williams: "No event has so corroborated my belief in the next life as Charles Williams did simply by dying. For when the idea of death and the idea of Williams thus met in my mind, it was the idea of death that was changed."

The weakness of this argument is the weakness of love itself: it is free, not a compulsion. If you do not choose to love, you will not see. But if you really want to know, you can perform the relevant experiment. The road to certainty about immortality can be an active experiment, not just a thought, and this can be more, not less, convincing than any theoretical argument. As Dostoyevsky's Father Zossima says in *Brothers Karamazov* to the "lady of little faith" who wonders how to regain her lost faith in immortality, "Insofar as you advance in love, you will grow surer of the reality of God and of the immortality of the soul. This has been tried. This is certain." The way is offered to all sincere seekers with the promise that if they really travel it, they will surely see.

The Argument from Christ's Resurrection

What would be the most convincing evidence for life after death? Skeptics would probably reply: Only if we could see and touch a dead man who had risen again and shown himself to us, could we be absolutely sure.

A dead man did rise and appear to many on this earth. The risen Christ was seen and touched (1 Jn 1:1-3). Christians are assured of life after death not through argument first of all but through witnesses. The Church is that chain of witnesses, beginning with the apostles.

Thus the Christian's answer to the most skeptical question of all, "What do you really know about life after death, anyway? Have you ever been there? Have you come back to tell us?" is "No, but I have a very good Friend who has."

12

Heaven and Hell

Next to the idea of God, the idea of heaven is the greatest idea that has entered the human mind. If it is denied and attacked more today than in the past, then the apologist had better explain and defend it better today than in the past and certainly not water it down or ignore it.

Even more difficult to defend than the idea of heaven is the idea of hell. Indeed, hell is probably the most difficult Christian doctrine to defend, the most burdensome to believe and the first to be abandoned. The critic's case against it seems very strong, and the believer's duty to believe it seems unbearable.

The focus of this chapter is to answer the objections of unbelievers against heaven and hell.

Heaven

We have outlined below seventeen objections to the idea of heaven. Our intent is not to provide a theology of heaven, nor is it to provide a picture of heaven intended for inspiration or personal edification. Much, much more remains to be said after the objections have been answered.

OBJECTION 1: *Reincarnation is more reasonable.*

Christians reject reincarnation for eight reasons.

1. It is contradicted by Scripture (Heb 9:27).
2. It is contradicted by orthodox tradition in all churches.
3. It implies that God made a mistake in designing our souls to live in bodies, that we are really pure spirits in prison or angels in costume.
4. It is contradicted by psychology and common sense, for its view of souls as imprisoned in alien bodies denies the natural psychosomatic unity.
5. It entails a very low view of the body, as a prison, a punishment.
6. The idea that we are reincarnated in order to learn lessons we failed to learn in a past earthly life is contrary to both common sense and basic educational psychology. I cannot learn something if there is no continuity of memory. I can learn from my mistakes only if I remember them. People do not usually remember these past "reincarnations."
7. The supposed evidence for reincarnation, rememberings from past lives that come out under hypnosis or "past life regression," can be explained—if they truly occur at all—as mental telepathy from other living beings, from the souls of dead humans in purgatory or hell, or from demons. The real possibility of the latter should make us extremely skittish about opening our souls to "past life regressions."
8. Reincarnation cannot account for itself. Why are our souls imprisoned in bodies? Is it the just punishment for evils we committed in past reincarnations? But why were those past reincarnations necessary? For the same reason. But the beginning of the process that justly imprisoned our souls in bodies in the first place must have antedated the series of

bodies. How could we have committed evil in the state of perfect, pure, heavenly spirituality? Further, if we sinned in that paradise, it is not paradisical after all. Yet that is the state that reincarnation is supposed to lead us back to after all our embodied yearnings are over.

OBJECTION 2: *There is no scientific evidence for heaven.*

Reply A: Nor for many other ideas that everyone admits are valid, even the scientist. When the scientist closes his laboratory and goes home and kisses his wife, he does not believe there is nothing there but hormones and neurons and molecules.

Reply B: There is no scientific evidence for the notion that nothing exists except what is proved by scientific evidence. The objector assumes that whatever there is no scientific evidence for does not exist (e.g., there is no scientific evidence for heaven, therefore heaven does not exist). But there is no scientific evidence for that assumption; it cannot be proved by the scientific method. It is simply an assumption; in fact, it is an arbitrary decision of will to narrow the bounds of reality to the bounds of the scientific method.

OBJECTION 3: *Heaven is obviously wishful thinking. If there were no heaven, we would have to invent it. It is a "necessary dream."*

Reply A: The heaven of the Bible does not correspond to our dreams or wishful thinking. It is selfless, self-forgetful love and saintliness, not the gratification of selfish desires.

Reply B: Even if there is a correspondence between our innate wishes and the idea of heaven, that correspondence could be explained equally well by God's having designed us for heaven rather than by our having designed heaven for ourselves. The glove could have been made for the hand, *or* the hand could have been made for the glove.

OBJECTION 4: *The very form, or structure, of the idea of heaven is mythic or legendary. The golden streets are just another version of the "happy hunting grounds" or the Elysian Fields.*

Reply A: Distinguish the imagery from the substance. To disbelieve in the substance because you mistook the imagery for literal description is as foolish as disbelieving in the moon because you mistook the "man in the moon" for a literal man.

Reply B: The fact that all religions and cultures have some version of heaven or paradise is evidence for, not against, its reality. If everyone (or nearly everyone) believes a story, only snobbery would conclude from that fact alone that the story is likely to be false rather than true.

OBJECTION 5: *Believing in heaven is escapist.*

Reply A: The most pointed answer to the charge of escapism is C. S. Lewis's simple question: "Who talks the most against 'escapism'? Jailers." Think about it.

Reply B: Is it escapist for an unborn baby to wonder about life after birth? Is it escapist for a pilgrim to wonder about his holy destination? Is it escapist for the shipwrecked sailor on a raft to dream of landfall? Is it escapist for the seed to dream of the flower? The caterpillar of the butterfly? Juliet of Romeo? Heaven is not escapist, because it is the fulfillment of all good earthly desires.

Reply C: Heaven is not escapist, because it is real. The idea is "escapist" only if it is a lie. To call the idea of heaven escapist is to presuppose atheism but not to have the clarity or courage to say so. If heaven is real, it is escapist *not* to think about it. It is *realistic* to do so.

The first question about any idea cannot be whether it is escapist but whether it is true. The label "escapist" is itself escapist; those who use it are trying to escape their primary obligation to prove the idea false.

OBJECTION 6: *Heaven is a diversion. Whether true or false, it distracts us from our present tasks.*

Reply A: Not if heaven is real. If it is, and if it is our ultimate destination, then our present tasks more often distract us from our primary task.

Reply B: Concern for heavenly things does not devalue or demean concern for earthly things for the same reason a pregnant woman's concern for her baby's future does not devalue, detract or distract from her concern for her baby's present. If she believed her baby was going to be born dead, or if she wanted her baby dead (i.e., wanted an abortion), *then* the baby's life would be demeaned and devalued, and she would cease to care for it. If we believe that this life ends with death, like a cosmic abortion, then we will care for it not more but less than if we believe that it is a pregnancy that will bear eternity.

The early roads that led to California and the gold mines were well paved and cared for. The roads that led to ghost towns were abandoned. If earth is the road to heaven, we will care for it. If it leads nowhere but to the ghost town of the grave, we will not.

Reply C: Throughout history, it has been those who believed most strongly in heaven who made the greatest difference to earth, including Jesus himself. For if you believe in the fatherland, you care for its colonies.

OBJECTION 7: *Heaven is a bribe. It makes religion selfish. You work for your heavenly reward, not for pure love. It's mercenary.*

Reply: Is it mercenary for Romeo to want to marry Juliet? For a team that has worked hard to want victory? For a student of a foreign language to want to read and speak it fluently? Some rewards are not mercenary but natural and right. They are not artificially tacked on to the activity they reward, like a grade in a course, but are that activity itself in its perfected state. Such is heaven. It is not some reward externally added to love of God and neighbor, but that love itself perfected.

OBJECTION 8: *Heaven is too egotistical. What arrogance to think you are destined to be spiritually married to God!*

Reply: God said it, not us. It is indeed amazing. God is amazing.

OBJECTION 9: *Heaven will be boring. Nothing to do but worship—an unending church service.*

Reply A: Boredom is a specifically earthly and fallen emotion. Even more, it is especially modern; a word for boredom in general does not exist in any premodern language. We will not be bored in heaven because we will be good and wise. Even here on earth, saints are never bored.

Reply B: Heaven will not be boring because it will not be merely contentment, which gets boring, but joy, which does not.

Reply C: Heaven is not boring because it is perfect love and work. Even Freud knew that the two things everyone needs to make life worth living are love and work.

What love-work will heaven be? The six love-works of knowing and loving God, others and yourself. Even on earth these are the six things that are inexhaustible and nonboring. They are our dress rehearsal for heaven.

OBJECTION 10: *How can we be happy in heaven if any of our loved ones are in hell? If we stop loving them, we are not good; if we keep loving them, we are not happy.*

Reply A: Let us begin with the data that we do know. We know that there will be no sadness in heaven, though we may not know *how* God manages this. God "will wipe every tear from their eyes. Death will be no more; mourning and crying and pain will be no more" (Rev 21:4).

God manages not to be sad, even though people he created and loves are in hell. God is infinite love and infinite joy, even though some go to hell. It *can* be done, because it *is* done: God does it. If God does it, he will teach us how to do it.

Reply B: If human beings were alive in hell, and heaven were parallel to hell in time as earth and Mars are parallel worlds, then there would seem to be no answer to the objection. But hell is a place of eternal death, not eternal life; and what goes to hell is what was once a human being but is now "remains" (see C. S. Lewis, *The Problem of Pain,* chap. 9). Nor are heaven and hell parallel worlds; you can't go from one to the other (Lk 16:26). Nor are they parallel in time. So all the implicit assumptions of the objection are false.

Reply C: If there are people you love and identify with so deeply that you simply cannot see how you could possibly be happy forever without them, then one of the jobs God may have put you on earth for is to do everything you can for their salvation as well as your own. Perhaps your concern is a clue to its answer: perhaps God has put that burden on your heart for you to work with him to lift it, to solve it.

OBJECTION 11: *Heaven is eternal. But eternity seems inhuman because without time there is no progress, no change, no work. Passive, changeless adoration seems fit for angels but not for us.*

Reply: Who says there is no time and work and change in heaven? Probably eternity includes all time rather than excluding it. Perhaps instead of only a tiny bit of time being present (what we now call "the present"), *all* of time is accessible in heaven's present. As to work, there is work in heaven, and that work is to love. Love is a work. Before the Fall, work was also a love. Only after the Fall did work become onerous (Gen 3:17-19). Heaven will restore and surpass all the good in paradise (Eden), including all the good in work, change and time.

OBJECTION 12: *Are we free to sin in heaven? If not, we are unfree robots, not free-willed humans. If so, heaven is dangerous, like earth. And if anyone there chooses to sin, it's Eden and the Fall and earth all over again.*

Reply: "Free to sin" is like "healthy disease." It means "freedom of enslavement."

Free will, or free choice, is the means to a higher freedom, or liberty. The lower freedom, the means, is freedom from compulsion. The higher freedom, the end, is the freedom from evil.

In heaven no one will sin because no one will want to. There, we will all see the beauty and joy and attractiveness of God and goodness, and the ugliness and joylessness and stupidity of sin, so clearly that there will be no possible motive to sin.

OBJECTION 13: *If we will all be perfect saints in heaven, where will individuality be? Billions of carbon copies of God seems dull.*

Reply A: Copies of each other are dull; copies of God are infinitely interesting. God is like a diamond with infinitely diverse facets. Each of the blessed reflects a different facet.

Reply B: Even now, the saints are the truest individuals. "How drearily alike are the great tyrants and sinners; how gloriously different the saints!" (C. S. Lewis, *Mere Christianity*).

Sanctity, letting God rule your soul and life, is like salt: it brings out the individual flavor of each of the different foods it flavors. It makes fish fishier, steak steakier and eggs eggier. It makes Augustine more Augustinian and Thomas more Thomistic, Teresa more Teresian and Mary more Marian.

OBJECTION 14: *If God's light and truth permeate heaven, there will be no privacy. That will be intolerable.*

Reply: Privacy—like clothes, locks and police officers—is needed now only because of sin. We hide from others because (a) we feel shame and (b) we fear others will misunderstand or reject us. In heaven there is no shame (for all sin is gone) and no misunderstanding or rejection by God or his saints. We will enjoy there the intimacy we fear (and yet long for) here.

OBJECTION 15: *Is there sex in heaven? If not, most people today will not want to go there. If so, it seems too earthly, too anthropomorphic.*

Reply A: That many will not want to go there says nothing against heaven, only against the nongoers.

Reply B: Of course there is sexuality in heaven. Sexuality, or sexual identity, is part of our divinely designed humanity and is not abolished but transformed. We will be "like angels" (Mt 22:30) not by being neutered but by not marrying.

Sex is first of all something we *are,* not something we *do.* If the question is whether we can "do it" (i.e., copulate) in heaven, the answer is probably the same as the answer to a six-year-old boy who asks whether he can play with his model airplanes while he makes love when he grows up.

Since we will have real bodies, it will be *possible,* just as it will be possible to eat; Christ did that in his resurrection body. But we will probably never give it a thought—not because it will seem shameful or silly or vulgar but because there will be infinitely more ecstatic pleasures at hand. Perhaps these pleasures will include some kind of total union with other souls of which physical intercourse is now a clumsy and confused foreshadowing. Don't lovers seek a total intimacy and oneness and always attain only a partial and temporary one?

OBJECTION 16: *To love heaven is to be a traitor to earth, leaving it behind like a rat leaving a sinking ship. It is disloyal.*

Reply: Unless the Bible lies, earth is not our home; heaven is. Disloyalty to *heaven* is the fault, not disloyalty to earth.

OBJECTION 17: *Heaven sounds so alien, far, other, threatening, "unfit for human habitation." Like trying on a weird outfit of clothes and saying, "It's just not me."*

Reply: The one thing you will certainly feel in heaven is that this is your home, this is what you were designed and made for. God is a good tailor; he fits the heavenly clothes perfectly to each of his customers.

Hell

Heaven is far more important than hell. We know much more about it, and it is meant to occupy our mind much more centrally. But in battle an army must rush to defend that part of the line which is most attacked or which seems the weakest, and this doctrine is under attack today. Each doctrine is important. Removing one stone from a pile and leaving all the others untouched is like removing a vital organ from a body; all the others are affected and eventually killed.

1. To believe there is no hell presupposes that both Scripture and the Church lie, for both clearly teach the reality of hell.
2. If Scripture and the Church do not lie about what Jesus said about hell, then it presupposes that *Jesus* is the liar. For he was far more explicit and adamant about hell than anyone else in Scripture.

   A Christian who does not believe in hell is a contradiction in terms, because a Christian is one who believes in Christ, and Christ is one who believes in hell. The only way to believe in Christ without believing in hell is to reconstruct Christ according to your own desires. (*He* wants to reconstruct you according to *his* desires!)

   If there is no hell, Christ is not only a deceptive teacher but a wicked one, for he terrifies us needlessly, falsely and harmfully.

   In fact, the kindest, gentlest, most loving and compassionate man who ever opened his mouth has warned us with the greatest seriousness, strenuousness and sternness about hell. That is the irrefutable argument for it.

3. If we drop hell because it is unbearable to us, that presupposes the principle that we can change whatever doctrines we find unbearable or unacceptable; in other words, that doctrine is negotiable. Christianity then becomes a human ideology, not a divine revelation.
4. If there is no hell, life's choices no longer make an infinite difference. The height of the mountain and the depth of the valley, the importance of winning and the importance of losing a war or a game—these two things measure each other. C. S. Lewis said he never met a person who had a lively belief in heaven who did not also have a lively belief in hell. "If a game is to be taken seriously, it must be possible to lose it" *(The Problem of Pain)*.
5. If there is no hell, then salvation is universal and automatic. If salvation is universal and automatic, then ultimately there is no free will. Free will and hell go together; scratch at the idea of free will and you will find underneath it the possibility of hell.
6. If there is no hell to be saved from, then Jesus is not our Savior, but only our teacher, prophet, guru or model.
7. If there is no hell, a religious indifference follows. If faith in Christ as Savior is not necessary, we should recall all the missionaries and apologize for all the martyrs. If there is no such thing as fire, fire departments are a distraction and a waste.
8. If salvation is automatic, Christ's sacrificial death was a stupid mistake, a tragic accident. (This idea is devastatingly satirized in C. S. Lewis's *The Great Divorce*, chap. 5.)
9. If there is no reason for believing in the detested doctrine of

hell, there is also no reason to believe in the most beloved doctrine in Christianity: that God is love. The beloved doctrine is the reason critics most frequently give for disbelieving the detested doctrine; yet the two stand on exactly the same foundation.

Why do we believe that God is love? Not by philosophical reasoning. What logic can prove that the perfect, self-contained, independent Reality, who has no needs, nevertheless loves these superfluous creatures of his so much that he became one of them to suffer and die for them?

How do we know that God is love? Not by observation of nature, any more than by philosophical reasoning. "Nature red in tooth and claw" does not manifest love.

Not by science. No experiment has ever verified divine love, or measured or weighed it or even observed it.

Not by conscience, for conscience is "hard as nails." Conscience tells us what is right and wrong and tells us we are absolutely obliged to do right and not wrong, but it does not tell us we are forgiven.

Not by history either. History does not move by universal love but by universal selfishness.

There is one and only one reason anyone ever came to the idea that God is love, mercy and forgiveness—and only one good proof that this idea is true. That reason is the character of God revealed in the Bible, culminating in Jesus Christ. The exact same authority that is our only authority for believing God is love also assures us that there is a hell. Either we accept both on the same ground or reject both on the same ground, for they stand on the same ground.

10. Many believe that since there is a hell, God must be a God of wrath and vengeance and hate. But this does not follow. It may be that the very love of God constitutes the sinner's torture in hell. That love would threaten and torture the

egotism that the damned sinners insist on and cling to. A small child in a fit of rage, sulking and hating his parents, may feel their hugs and kisses at that moment as torture. By the same psychological principle, the massive beauty of an opera may be torture to someone blindly jealous of its composer. So the fires of hell may be made of the very love of God, or rather by the damned's hatred of that love.

"The wrath of God" is a scriptural expression. But (a) it is probably a metaphor, an anthropomorphic image, like "God's strong right hand" or God changing his mind. It is not literal. And (b) if it is not a metaphor but literal wrath (hate), it is a projection of our own hate onto God rather than a hate within God himself. And (c) if it is an objective fact in God rather than a subjective projection from us, then it refers to God's holiness and justice, not a smoldering resentment; it is his wrath against sin, not against sinners. God practices what he preaches to us: love sinners, hate sins. For surgeons to love their patients, they must hate their patients' cancers. The damned are those who refuse to dissociate themselves from their sins by repenting. Every sin must meet its necessary fate: exclusion from heaven. Only if we glue ourselves to our sins do we glue ourselves to that fate.

God is perfect mercy and forgiveness. But let us be clear about what that means. Forgiveness appeals to freedom; it must be freely given and freely accepted, like any gift. If we do not repent and ask for God's forgiveness, we do not receive it—not because God holds it back but because we hold ourselves back.

11. Some have taught or implied that hell is forced on the damned, that they are thrown into hell against their will. This would go contrary to the fundamental reason for hell's existence: our free choice and God respecting it.

The damned in hell do not *enjoy* hell, but they do *will* it, by willing egotism instead of love, self instead of God, sin instead of repentance. There can be no heaven without self-giving love. The thing the damned wish for—happiness on their own selfish terms—is impossible even for God to give. It does not exist. It cannot exist.

12. If hell is chosen freely, the problem then becomes not one of reconciling hell with God's love but reconciling hell with human sanity. Who would freely prefer hell to heaven unless they were insane?

    The answer is that all of us do at one time or another. Every sin reflects that preference.

13. Perhaps the worst exaggeration of hell is the Calvinistic doctrine (not even held by all Calvinists) of a double predestination. According to this doctrine, God decrees and designs some souls for hell before they are born; God *wills* their damnation. This is contradicted both by Scripture (Mt 18:14) and by moral sanity; how could one love such a monster God?

    There is indeed a predestination to heaven, like an AAA road map plotting the right road for your happy vacation. The words *destined* and *predestination* are right there in Scripture (Rom 8:29-30; Eph 1:5, 11). We think the *pre* has to be interpreted nonliterally, since God is not in time. But the crucial point is what kind of God God is. We must not think that because there is a hell, God is like a divine concentration camp commander who capriciously sends some to the gas chambers and spares others. Christians believe God himself has told them how to think of him, and they always bear in mind his images of love: father, good shepherd, mother hen (Mt 23:37).

The Proper Use and Misuse of the Doctrine of Hell

Most passionate objections to the doctrine of hell are really objections to those religious teachers who have misused it. (This seems especially prevalent among American fundamentalists and Irish Catholics.) The objection comes down to this: hell was probably invented out of hate, fear and the desire to control and dominate people, since that is the fruit the doctrine produces.

The same objection, however, can be lodged against the doctrine of heaven: that it is misused, produces an irresponsible lack of concern for this world and manipulates people like a carrot on a stick. In fact, *any* idea, true or false, can be misused and abused. This tells us nothing about its truth or a falsity.

Why must we believe in and teach hell? First, for the only good reason to believe or teach anything: because it is true, because it is there. In other words, out of honesty. Second, out of love, out of compassion, out of the fear that love generates that any loved and precious soul end up there by disbelieving the warning signs, like children drowning because the ice seemed thick enough and the warning signs were ignored. When there is real war, the *least* loving thing we can do is to cry "peace, peace when there is no peace" (Jer 8:11).

Those who preach this truth will be hated and feared, mocked and maligned, as fools, sadists or manipulators. So be it. Christians today are often more terrified of sharing their Lord's holy unpopularity than of hell itself. (You don't nail a man to a cross for telling you things you like to hear!) To be called a nasty name is a small price to pay for the privilege of possibly contributing one strand to the rope that saves an infinitely precious little one for whom Christ died.

13

Salvation

One of the most unforgettable bishops in New York's history electrified the large audience in the Bronx at his inaugural speech many ago. He had been preceded by a typical "brick and mortar" administrator, fundraiser, organizer and "nice guy." But the new bishop announced, "I am here for one reason and one only. Everything I do for you will have one single aim: to save your souls." Unfortunately, most of the people had never heard anyone say that before.

The only justification for every dollar raised, every Bible or hymnbook printed, every speck of dust swept up from under every pew, is salvation: union with God (*theosis* in Eastern Orthodox terminology). That is the business the Church is in.

The Church also seems to be in the social service business, the counseling business, the fundraising business, the daycare business—dozens of the same worthy businesses the secular world is also in. Why? What justifies these things? The Church's ultimate end for all these things is different from the world's end; it is salvation. This is its distinctive "product."

Why put out a product that is just the same as other companies' products already on the market? Why would anyone expect such a product to sell? That's why modernist or liberal Christianity, charitable as its services are, is simply not selling. The only reason for any of the Church's activities, the only reason for the very existence of the Church at all, is exactly the same as the reason Jesus came to earth: to save poor and lost humanity. The Church, after all, is in the same business as its Head.

Jesus did not come to be a philosopher or a doctor. If he did that, he failed. He didn't solve most of the philosophers' problems. He healed some people, but left most of the world just as sick as before. He healed some bodies to show that he could heal all souls.

Not only is salvation the reason for the Church's existence, it is also the ultimate reason for your existence: your end, goal, point, purpose, hope, final cause, *summum bonum,* meaning. The difference between success and failure at life's first task—becoming who you were meant to be—is not the difference between riches and poverty, fame and obscurity, health and sickness, pleasure and pain, or niceness and nastiness, but between salvation and damnation. Leon Bloy wrote, "There is only one tragedy: not to have been a saint." Jesus said, "What does it profit a man if he gains the whole world but loses his soul?" No one in history ever asked a more practical question than that one. In other words, don't get all A's but flunk life.

That is why ordinary people, as distinct from scholars, always ask questions about salvation whenever they think about religion. And that's why a book on apologetics must address this topic; it's what religion is for.

Faith and Works

The issue of salvation sparked the Protestant Reformation and split the Church. It seemed to both sides at the time that Protestants and Catholics taught two radically different gospels, two religions, two answers to the most basic of all questions: What must I do to be saved? Catholics said you must both believe *and* practice good works to be saved. Luther, Calvin, Wycliffe and Knox insisted that faith alone saves you. Unfortunately, both sides have been talking past each other for 450 years. But there is strong evidence that it was essentially a misunderstanding and that it is beginning to be cleared up.

Both sides used key terms, *faith* and *salvation,* but in different senses.

1. Catholics used the term *salvation* to refer to the whole process, from its beginning in faith, through the whole Christian life of the works of love on earth, to its completion in heaven. When Luther spoke of *salvation* he meant the initial step—like getting into Noah's ark.
2. By *faith* Catholics meant only one of the three needed "theological virtues" (faith, hope and love), faith being intellectual belief. To Luther, *faith* meant accepting Christ with your whole heart and soul.

Thus, since Catholics were using *salvation* in a bigger sense and *faith* in a smaller sense, and Luther was using *salvation* in a smaller sense and *faith* in a bigger sense, Catholics rightly denied and Luther rightly affirmed that we were saved by faith alone.

Catholics taught that salvation included more than faith, just as a plant includes more than its roots. It needs its stem (hope) and its fruits (love) as well as its root (faith). Luther taught that good works can't buy salvation, that all you need to do and all you *can* do to be saved is to accept it, accept the Savior, by faith. Both were right.

Such real agreement in substance beneath apparent disagreement in words should not be surprising, for both Catholics and Protestants accept the same data, the New Testament.

The New Testament teaches both points: that salvation is a free gift, not earned by works of obedience to the law; and that faith is only the beginning of the Christian life of good works; that "justification" (being made right with God) must, if it is; real, lead to "sanctification" (being made holy, saintly, good), that "faith without works is dead."

Sincerity Not Sufficient

QUESTION: *Why should God demand faith in Jesus for a person to be saved? What more does God want than a sincere heart?*

Reply: No one accepts sincerity alone as sufficient in any other field than religion. Sincerity may be *necessary* but it is no *sufficient.* Is it sufficient that your surgeon, your accountant o your travel agent be sincere? Is sincerity alone enough to save you from cancer, bankruptcy, accident or death? It is not. Why then do you think it should be enough to save you from hell?

The assumption behind this objection comes from the single most important change in religious thought in the last nineteen hundred years. Whereas nearly all the ancients (not just the Christians) believed that religion is about objective truth, just as medicine or economics or geography are about objective truth, most typical moderns do not. (See chapter fifteen on objective truth.)

Moderns typically see religion in four radically different ways from nearly all premoderns.

1. Moderns see religion as subjective rather than objective; as something in us and our consciousness rather than as something that we and our consciousness are in. Modern religious educators talk less about God than about our religious experience and practice.
2. Moderns see religion as only practical rather than theoretical, only good rather than true, only moral rather than theological, only a pattern for living rather than a map of reality. Thus

it becomes pragmatic and relativistic: if it works for you, use it.

3. Moderns see religion as something made by us rather than by God; something we create rather than discover; our road to God rather than God's road to us.

4. Moderns see religion as an addition rather than subtraction; as self-growth rather than self-death; as exercise rather than surgery. For the typically modern mind does not believe in the disease called sin. But sincerity alone is not enough to take away sin, any more than it is enough to take away cancer. You need a real doctor. You can't do it yourself. You need more than sincerity; you need a Savior.

Can Non-Christians Be Saved?

Whether we answer yes or no to the question whether non-Christians can be saved, we seem to be in a dilemma. If we answer no, the objection fairly leaps out: Then all non-Christians go to hell, even a good pagan like Socrates. It wasn't his fault that he didn't live in the right time or place to meet Jesus or a Christian missionary. How unfair and unloving of God to consign most of the world to hell! If we reply that non-Christians like Socrates can be saved, then the question naturally arises: Why then become a Christian? If whatever Socrates had is enough to get to heaven, why add the narrow claim about Jesus being the only way? In other words, if Socrates is not in heaven, God is not just, and if Socrates is in heaven, then Jesus is not the only way there.

Objective salvation versus subjective knowledge of salvation. The dilemma is not just a tricky, technical, theological problem; it is about the most important of all questions, "What must I do to be saved?" To answer it, we need to make a crucial distinction between the objective and the subjective dimensions of the question. The New Testament gives a clear, uncompromising and narrow answer to the objective question, but not to the subjective question.

Objectively, the New Testament insists that Christ is the only Savior. Jesus himself insisted, "I am *the* way. . . . No one comes to the Father except through me" (Jn 14:6). Christians believe Jesus is the only Savior because he said so. If this is not true, he is no Savior at all, but a liar, a blasphemer and an incredibly egotistical fool.

Subjectively, what do we need to be saved? The New Testament says we need faith in him to be saved, but what does this mean? What kind of faith? There cannot be different kinds of Jesus, but there *may* be different kinds of faith. The line between Jesus and all others is clearly drawn; the line between the faith of Peter and the possible faith of Socrates is not so clear.

What might it mean to say Socrates could have had faith in Christ? To have faith in Christ, you must somehow know Christ. How could Socrates have known Christ? In the same way everyone can: as "the true light, which enlightens everyone" (Jn 1:9); as the preincarnate Logos, the divine Word or Light or Reason.

No one can know God except through Christ (Jn 1:18; Lk 10:22). But pagans know God (Acts 17:28; Rom 1:19-20; 2:11-16). Therefore pagans know Christ. For Christ is not just a six-foot-tall, thirty-three-year-old Jewish carpenter. He is the second person of the eternal Trinity, the full expression, or revelation, or Logos, of the Father (Col 1:15, 19; Jn 14:9). Thus, the doctrine of Christ's divinity—classified as "conservative" or "traditionalist" by liberals—is the very foundation of the liberals' hope that pagans may be saved.

Explicit knowledge of the incarnate Jesus is not necessary for salvation. Abraham, Moses and Elijah, for instance, had no such knowledge, yet they were saved. (We know that from Mt 17:3 and Lk 16:22-23.) The same person—the second person of the Trinity—is both the preincarnate Logos who "enlightens everyone" *and* the incarnate Jesus who was seen only by some. *Those who know either one know the other too, because both are the same person.*

To summarize our solution: Socrates (or any other pagan)

could seek God, could repent of his sins, and could obscurely believe in and accept the God he knew partially and obscurely, and therefore he could be saved—or damned, if he refused to seek, repent and believe. There is enough light and enough opportunity, enough knowledge and enough free choice, to make everyone responsible before God. God is just. And a just God judges justly, not unjustly; that is, he judges according to the knowledge each individual has, not according to a knowledge they do not have (see Jas 3:1).

The objection to the salvation of pagans. Conservatives often object that this position, which allows the possibility for pagans to be saved, undercuts the motivation for mission work. Why spend your life, why risk your life, to tell the world about Jesus if people can be saved without that knowledge? It is a good question, and it deserves a good answer.

There are three possible reasons for mission work, that is, for telling others the gospel, the "good news" of Jesus. (By the way, all Christians are commanded to be missionaries; the Great Commission [Mt 28:18-20] did not come with a "clergy only" tag.) First, there is the reason given by many fundamentalists: We know that the world is going to hell unless they accept Christ as their Savior. Second, there is the reason given by many modernists: We just want to love our neighbor and share whatever we have with them, do a sort of super social work. We don't believe in hell, and if we did, we wouldn't think anyone went there, and if they did, we'd think it was only a Hitler or a Stalin. We are not in the salvation business, we are in the social service business. Third, there is the traditional reason: We do *not* know exactly who is on the way to hell, that's why we risk all to save some. A mother doesn't need to know that her children are going to fall through the thin ice and drown before she is motivated to shout, "Get off the ice!" All she needs to know is that she *doesn't* know that they *won't* drown, that they *may* drown. We know that anyone *may* go to hell, because Jesus said so. So we are not modernists. But we do not know exactly *which* children are going to be lost, because Jesus didn't tell us. So we shout the warning and throw out the life preserver just as insistently as the fundamentalists.

There is a parallel here with abortion. There are three possible attitudes to abortion, parallel to the three reasons given above for mission work, distinguished by what you claim to know. Some claim to know that the soul enters the body at conception, making the fetus a person, and therefore that abortion is murder. Some claim to know that this is *not* true and therefore that abortion is not murder. And some do not claim to know when the soul enters the body, when the fetus becomes a person. Though this skeptical claim is most often found among prochoice people, it is a compelling reason for being prolife. If you don't know for sure that an unborn baby is not a person and has no soul, how horribly callous and irresponsible to risk the possibility of murder! It's like shooting a gun into a busy city street, or running over a human-shaped pile of clothes with a truck.

Ignorance and risk can be as compelling reasons for action as knowledge and certainty. If you think your child may be dying, you will rush to the doctor at the same speed as if you *know* your child is dying. Thus, the open-minded skepticism of the liberal and the passionate total commitment of the fundamentalist are perfectly compatible.

There is something more to be said about the motivation for mission work that is more important than all this calculation of possibility. Our motive for preaching the gospel is not only to increase the population of heaven and decrease the population of hell but also to invite others to a deeper spiritual life in *this* world: intimate knowledge and love of Christ that brings deep trust, hope, joy and peace. Without an explicit knowledge of Christ it is probably impossible to have these. And without them, though salvation may be possible, the *assurance* of salvation is not.

Postscript

It is important to make clear that we are *not* claiming here to know that Socrates has been saved, or that any, many or most pagans will be saved. We ask fundamentalists or evangelicals who find this position too "liberal" to first be sure exactly what our position is. We have said repeatedly that we simply do not know who or how many will be saved.

On the other hand, we ask liberals who are impatient with all this kowtowing to fundamentalists to consider how "liberal" their impatience really is, and to reexamine their own motives for rejecting the clear and repeated teaching of the only Christ we know. A love of believers in other religions and an appreciation for whatever true and good things there may be in these other religions should not blind us to their errors and defects. If Christ is the only Savior and all the other religions of the world deny this, then logically and necessarily all the other religions are dead wrong about this crucial point. It does not follow from this that non-Christians must be condemned, but that they must be told the truth, out of love for them *and* for the truth.

14

Christianity and Other Religions

In teaching apologetics and philosophy of religion for many years, we have found that students worry more and are more embarrassed by Christianity's "un-American" exclusivist claims than about any other aspect of their religion. In an age of toleration and pluralism, the most popular argument against the Christian religion seems to be simply that it is only one of many religions. The world is a big place; "different strokes for different folks"; "live and let live"; "don't impose your values on others."

The real religion of most Americans is equality; that is their absolute, self-evident value. God *must* be an American, an equal-opportunity employer. All religious roads, if only followed sincerely, must equally lead to God.

This way of thinking is very comfortable and seems very enlightened—until someone starts to think logically and ask obvious, hard questions like, Does that include Jim Jones's road to Jonestown? Satanism? Where do you draw the line?

Defining the Issues

We must distinguish at least five different questions about the Christian position regarding other religions:

1. Are they true?

2. Are they good (moral)?

3. Are they salvific? (Can they save you?)

4. Are they educative ? (Can Christians learn from them?)

5. Are they useful? (Should Christians practice things in them?)

Are other religions true? We cannot address this question until we agree on what is meant by "true." (See "Conclusion: The Bottom Line," p. 139). If we use the definition that is commonsensical in the West, namely, correspondence with objective reality, then the correct answer seems to be, Partly. (But as we shall see in a moment, other religions, especially Eastern religions, have a different definition of truth.)

We could say, for instance, that Vedanta Hinduism is true in being monotheistic and false in being pantheistic, or that Islam's insistence on prayer and justice are true, but its denial that God can have a Son is false.

But the very meaning of *truth* changes when you move East. For a pantheist the difference between truth and falsity cannot be the difference between the conformity and the nonconformity of the subjective mind to objective reality. For reality to a pantheist is one, not two; truth is not an idea's *conformity* but its *size*, so to speak. Only the idea of Oneness or Brahman or Nirvana is totally "true"; all lesser ideas are partly true and partly false, partial manifestations of the Whole.

This makes argument between East (Hinduism, Buddhism, Taoism) and West (Judaism, Christianity, Islam) extremely difficult. For the West claims that the East is wrong on some points, and the East claims that there is no such thing as being wrong. A Hindu can believe everything, including Christianity, as a partial truth, or a stage along the way to total truth. Even contradictory ideas can be accepted as true; the stumbling block of East-West dialogue is the law of noncontradiction.

The East's argument is that its notion of truth includes the West's, but not vice versa; that the East is inclusive, the West exclusive. This is probably the main reason for the great popularity of Eastern religions in the West today, especially on an informal, unofficial level. Not many Americans are Hindus, but most prefer the Hindu notion of truth to the Western one, at least in religion.

But the real situation is just the opposite: the traditional West includes the East, not vice versa. The West already understands the Eastern insight that there is such a thing as degrees of truth (i.e., degrees of understanding, insight, depth, adequacy, wisdom). But the West adds that there is also such a thing as the law of noncontradiction. Contradictory propositions cannot both be true in the same sense at the same time. The East does not admit this.

For instance, suppose there are many degrees of depth in understanding the meaning of the word *God.* Even so, either God has a will and wills a moral law, as the West believes, or else not, as the East believes. It can't be both. It is the East that fails to see the West's insight here, that truth is more than just the degree of understanding of a term's meaning; it is also the either-or matter of a proposition's being correct or incorrect, matching or mismatching reality.

Using this Western meaning of truth, our answer to the question "Are other religions true?" is "Certainly, in part." Even Satan has to speak some truth in order to sell his lies. Satan tells Satanists some truths (e.g., that Satan is real and powerful and wants us to commit crimes like the ritual sacrifice of babies). How much more, then, will we find many truths in wise and humane and enlightened teachers like Buddha, Confucius and Muhammad. It remains to be seen, however, how their truths compare with Christianity's, and how and whether they are mixed with falsehoods.

The only "other" religion Christians accept as *wholly* true is biblical Judaism, for the simple reason that this is not an "other" religion at all but the foundation of Christianity. Christ said, "Do not think that I have come to abolish the law or the prophets; I have come not to abolish but to fulfill" (Mt 5:17). Christians believe everything Jews believe and more, just as Catholics believe everything orthodox, biblical Protestants believe and more. Modern Jews fault Christians for believing too many things, just as Protestants fault Catholics for believing too many things.

Are other religions good? What of the ethics, the morality of other religions? With the exception of Satanic religion(s), every religion in the world has not only some but a lot of true morality. The moral codes of the world's great religions are not nearly as different as their theologies. You can even find many of the values Jesus taught in the Sermon on the Mount in Plato, Confucius, Lao-tzu or Buddha, though not in the same context of a historical "kingdom of God."

There are some significant ethical contradictions between religions, however, based on their different theological beliefs. For instance, suppose you were a typical Hindu. You would believe that (a) this body is ultimately only an appearance; (b) we must all work out our karma, or moral fate; and (c) after death everyone except a fully enlightened mystic must go through many more reincarnations. For these reasons, you would not be swift to rescue a dying derelict from the gutter. For (a) bodily death is not very important; (b) you may be interfering with the person's karma, or fated learning experience through this suffering and dying; and (c) death is not terribly tragic because it is not final—we go round again and may get other chances through reincarnation.

If, on the other hand, you were a Christian or a Jew or a

Muslim, you would act like the good Samaritan because you believe that (a) the body is real and good and important; (b) we are not fated but free (or both fated and free); and (c) we live only once, so life is incalculably precious.

However, such moral disagreements as these are unusual. More often there is not only agreement but remarkable agreement. Moral codes can be classified into three levels: codes for pragmatic survival, codes of objective justice and codes of selflessness. All three tell us not to bash each other's brains out, but for three different reasons: not to get bashed back; because it's not fair; and because we should be unselfish like God, or the Ultimate Reality. Everyone knows level one, and most civilized people know level two, but level three is high and rare. Yet *all* the great religions of the world teach level three morality.

Are other religions salvific? Can other religions save you? So far, our answers have been rather liberal: there is much truth and much moral goodness in other religions. Now we will begin to sound very conservative. Christianity cannot get rid of its founder's claim to be the only Savior.

However, as we have seen in chapter thirteen, the doctrine that Christ is the only Savior does not necessarily entail the conclusion that consciously professing Christians are the only ones saved. Passages like Romans 1 and John 1:9 tell us that God shines light into everyone's mind and speaks to all people through conscience, God's inner microphone. Christians do not claim to know how many people respond to this knowledge of God in such a way as to be saved; but they do claim to know (because Jesus has told them) that if and when and however anyone is saved, it must be by Jesus, the one and only Savior.

Christianity's exclusive claims are not for Christianity but for Christ. Christians, by definition, believe Christ to be God-made-man, God-in-the-flesh. His claims cannot be amended, watered down, relativized, negotiated away or nuanced into acceptability.

But this exclusivism is not an exclusivism of Christian culture, of Christian ethics or of Christians as the only candidates for heaven. Attacks on Christian exclusivism often ignorantly or maliciously confuse these three indefensible exclusivisms with the real one, which is almost never squarely faced. (How often have you heard any non-Christian face the central question of whether Jesus' claims for himself are true or false?)

Are other religions educative? Can Christians learn any wisdom from other religions? Certainly! Our own Scriptures tell us that the God who spoke in many and various ways to our Jewish fathers (Heb 1:1) has not left himself without a witness among the Gentile nations (Acts 17:22-28; Rom 1:19-20).

There are at least three good reasons for Christians to study other religions.

1. To appreciate our own religion better by contrast.
2. To reinforce and deepen our understanding of similar aspects of our own religion. For instance, Confucius can teach us much about practical social, moral and cosmic harmony; Lao-tzu about God's quiet, invisible, yielding power in nature; Buddha about the importance of silence and meditation; and, above all, Muhammad, about submission *(islam)* to God and his will. However, great caution and discernment are needed, especially if these teachings are not just studied from without but integrated into one's life from within.
3. To seek and find truth wherever it may be. All truth is God's truth. We do not know where truth is until we look. So we should look everywhere, if we value truth, like a parent in search of precious children.

Are other religions useful? Should a Christian use some Zen Buddhist meditation techniques? Should Chinese Christians use Confucius as their teacher of social ethics? Should Christian pacifists learn from Gandhi's methods? Should Jewish Christians celebrate the Jewish holidays?

Such questions should be addressed with great care, for religion is the active, actual service of God, gods, spirits or demons. Before Christians use a mantra from a Transcendental Meditation teacher, they should be sure it is not the name of a demon, camouflaged—because it usually *is!* Before opening up their spirit to meditation, they should be sure it opens up to God, not to nothingness—because in Zen there is no difference! Discernment is needed, on a case-by-case basis. Indiscriminate inclusion or indiscriminate exclusion are equally unthinking.

On the one hand, we must remember that Eastern methods have been developed as means to non-Christian ends; and there is an organic connection between means and ends. The Eastern end is mysticism; sanctity is only a means. The Christian (and Jewish and Muslim) end is sanctity; mysticism is only a means to or a result of this higher end. For a Hindu or Buddhist, sanctity only purifies the individual soul so that it can see through itself as an illusion. For Christians, mysticism is only a reward of sanctity or a motor for more sanctity.

Christ tells us to love God; Hindus tell us we *are* God. Christ tells us to love our neighbor; Buddha tells us we *are* our neighbor. The Eastern goal is to see through the illusions of ego, soul, body, self, other, matter, space, time, world, good, evil, true, false, beautiful, ugly, this and that. The Christian goal is to know, love, please, serve, marry and enjoy God in this life and the next.

On the other hand, while the Bible tells us a lot about the second half of its own command to "be still and know that I am God," it tells us very little about how to do the first. In principle, some natural and neutral Eastern techniques might be separated from Eastern ends and enlisted in the service of that Christian end.

It is the saints, not just the theologians, who will be our leaders in discernment here.

The most important issue in "comparative religions" is not

the abstract and general issues above but the concrete and specific issue of the identity of Jesus. The field of "comparative religions" has given those who do not want to accept Jesus' claim to be divine another detour off the road that leads to him, one last possible escape from the argument for his divinity presented in chapter eight. Perhaps Jesus is neither Lord nor liar nor lunatic nor myth but a guru.

According to this theory, we should interpret his claim to divinity not in a Western, Jewish or Christian sense but in an Eastern, Hindu or Buddhist sense. Yes, Jesus was God, and knew it, and claimed it—but we are all God. We unenlightened nonmystics just don't realize it. Jesus was an enlightened mystic, a guru, who realized his own inner divinity. There are thousands of people today, as in the past, who claim to be God but are neither liars nor lunatics. They are gurus, yogis, roshis, "spiritual masters," "enlightened" mystics. Why couldn't Jesus fit into this well-established and well-populated class?

For one very simple reason: because he was a Jew. No guru was ever a Jew and no Jew was ever a guru. The differences—more, the contradictions—between the religious Judaism of Jesus and the teaching of all the gurus, Hindu, Buddhist, Taoist or New Age, are so many, so great and so obvious that you have to be a dunce or a professor to miss them. It is utterly unhistorical, uprooted and deracinated to see Jesus as a Hindu and not a Jew; as a kind of generic, universal type of "enlightened consciousness." You cannot ignore his Jewishness.

If Jesus was in fact a guru or mystic who transcended and contradicted his Jewishness, then he utterly failed to get any one of the gurus' teachings across to anybody, ever, for almost two thousand years. He was the worst teacher in history if he misled all his followers on every one of the following essential points where Judaism and Eastern mysticism conflict.

1. Judaism is an exoteric (public) religion of collective obser-

vance of a public law (Torah) and belief in a public book (the Scriptures). But the gurus and mystics of all cultures teach an esoteric (private), individual, inner experience that cannot be communicated in words.

2. The Eastern mystics or gurus believe in a pantheistic, immanent God. For them, "enlightenment" consists in the realization that we and everything else are all, ultimately, God.

   Judaism's distinctive doctrine of God is that God is distinct from the world. He created it out of nothing. There is an infinite gap between Creator and creature. To confuse or identify a creature with the Creator is idolatry, a terrible sin.

   If a Hindu announced to his guru, "I just discovered that I am God," the response would be "Congratulations. You finally found out." If a Jew had said that two thousand years ago, the response would have been stoning (Jn 8:31-59) or crucifixion (Jn 19:1-7).

3. For Jews, God is a *person.* The supreme revelation of God was to Moses in the burning bush when he told Moses his own true eternal name: "I AM." For Jews "I" is the name of Ultimate Reality—God.

   For the gurus, "I" is the name of ultimate illusion. Individuality, personality, selfhood is the supreme illusion which must be seen through and dispelled if we are to attain the supreme truth of enlightenment. Far from being the nature of ultimate reality in God, it is not even real in us.

4. For the mystics, time and history are also ultimately unreal, illusory, projections of unenlightened consciousness. Enlightenment consists of emancipation from time. Salvation is found in timelessness. But for the Jews, time and matter (which are relative to each other) are real because God created them. For Judaism, God is known and loved and served within time. Judaism is a historical religion.

   For the mystic, salvation consists in going back beyond the

birth of the ego to the realization of our primordial identity with all things. But for the Jews, salvation consists in God doing his thing ("the Day of the Lord") in the future, in time, in history, in the messianic age. Mystics look away from time or back; Jews look at time and forward.

5. Mystics believe God is unknowable, except wordlessly in mystical experience. Jews believe God made himself known publicly in deeds and words, divinely inspired writings.
6. For the Jews, God is the active initiator. That is why he is always imaged as male—as king, husband, warrior. (Another reason is his transcendence; see the end of chapter four.) Religion is not our search for God but God's search for us.
7. The Jewish God is a moralist. He himself is moral, righteous, holy; and his command to us is "Be holy, for I am holy." He gives commandments. He has a will. He discriminates. He hates evil and loves good.

   The pantheistic God of the gurus has no will, no law, no preferences. He is totally nondiscriminating, like modern amoral Westerners. For the gurus, morality is at best a preliminary for enlightenment, a means to free the mind from passion (and love); at worst it is a dualistic illusion. It is our invention, not God's. Their God is "beyond good and evil."
8. Another major reason why Eastern religions are so popular among modern ex-Jews and ex-Christians is that they have no hell. There may be temporary purgatories—for example, reincarnations in this life and *bardos* in the next *(The Tibetan Book of the Dead)*—but everyone automatically gets to heaven eventually. The God of the gurus does not judge or punish sin. There is no sin, no separation from God, for God is the All.

   Biblical and orthodox Judaism, like Christianity, teaches an eternal, ultimate justice and judgment. Not everyone is automatically guaranteed salvation. The existence of hell logically follows from two other distinctively Judeo-Christian doctrines: the distinction between the Creator and the creature, and human free will. Pantheists cannot believe in hell because for them there is nothing but God, there can be no being apart from God. Determinists do not believe in hell because we are not free to choose it. Orthodox Jews and Christians believe in the possibility of hell (eternal separation from God) because we are not parts of God, and we are free to reject him. Which side is Jesus on? Jesus clearly, strongly and evidently believed in hell, and talked a lot about it.

So we have eight flat-out contradictions, all of them crucially important, between the teaching of Jesus as we have it in the New Testament and the teaching of the Eastern mystics and gurus. To classify Jesus as a guru is as accurate as classifying Marx as a capitalist.

15

Objective Truth

From a practical point of view, the question of whether we can know objective truth is one of the most important questions in apologetics, because today most arguments between Christians and non-Christians eventually come down to this point. What usually happens is this: After the Christian has won the substantive argument, the non-Christian, unable to refute the Christian's argument, retreats to this ubiquitous line of defense: "What you say may be true for you, but not for me. Truth is relative. What right do you have to impose your beliefs on me? You're being judgmental."

Christian apologetic strategy must be ready to cope with this move. We must be prepared to show our opponents (i.e., our friends) that they take refuge in this relativism and subjectivism only after they have lost the argument, never after they have won it, or think they have won it.

The consequences of a subjectivism and relativism of truth are destructive not only to apologetics but also to intellectual honesty and to life. For if truth is objective, if we live in a world we did not create and cannot change merely by thinking, if the world is not really a dream of our own, then the most destructive belief we could possibly believe would be the denial of this primary fact. It would be like closing your eyes while driving, or blissfully ignoring the doctor's warnings (C. S. Lewis, "The Poison of Subjectivism," in *Christian Reflections*).

Of all the symptoms of decay in our decadent civilization, subjectivism is the most disastrous of all. A mistake can possibly be discovered and amended if and only if truth exists and can be known and is loved and searched for. If a surgeon closes his eyes to the light in the operating room, there is no chance at all that the operation will work and that the patient will be saved.

Definition of *Objective*

1. The word *objective* in the phrase "objective truth" does not refer to an unemotional, detached or impersonal attitude. Truth is not an attitude. Truth is not *how* we know, truth is *what* we know.
2. *Objective* does not mean "known by all" or "believed by all." Even if everyone believes a falsehood, it is still false. "You don't find truth by counting noses."
3. *Objective* does not mean "publicly proved." An objective truth could be privately known—for example, the location of a hidden treasure. It could also be *known* without being *proved;* to know is one thing, to give good proofs or reasons for your knowledge is another.

What *objective* means in "objective truth" is "independent of the knower and his consciousness." "I itch" is a subjective truth; "Plato wrote the Republic" is an objective truth. "I don't want to be unselfish" is a subjective truth; "I ought to be unselfish whether I want to or not" is an objective truth.

Definition of *Truth*

In a sense, the whole issue between the subjectivist and the objectivist is the definition of *truth.* The definition we offer here is commonsensical; it is what most people and cultures in all times and places mean by *truth.* But the subjectivist would not agree with our definition. The definition itself is an "objectivist" one. So the issue is right here in the definition. We shall therefore compare and evaluate five alternative definitions of *truth* after giving the right one.

Aristotle, the master of common sense in philosophy, defined what ordinary people mean by *truth* as "saying of what is that it is and of what is not that it is not." *Truth* means the correspondence of what you know or say to what is. *Truth* means "telling it like it is."

Alternative Theories of Truth

1. ***The pragmatic theory of truth:*** "Truth is what works."

   Since "what works" is subjective and relative (what you *think* works, or what works *for you*), pragmatism is a form of subjectivism and relativism.

   Chesterton refuted pragmatism by saying that "man's most pragmatic need is to be something more than a pragmatist." For without an end, no one will work for any practical means. "Means" means "means-to-an-end." Without a more-than-pragmatic end, no one can be pragmatic. Pragmatism doesn't work; it isn't practical.

2. ***The empiricist theory of truth:*** "Truth is what we can sense."

   Empiricism as a theory of truth seems designed a priori, from the beginning, rather than empirically and from experience, to eliminate soul, spirit, God, heaven and objective moral law from the realm of objective truths.

   Empiricism itself is not an empirical, experimental, expe riential report on how we do in fact use words (like *spirit*), instead, it is a rationalistic, a priori ideological doctrine. Empiricism is not empirical enough.

3. ***The rationalist theory of truth:*** "Truth is what can be clearly and distinctly understood by reason," or "truth is what can be proved by reason."

   Just as pragmatism is unpragmatic and empiricism is not empirical, rationalism is irrational. You can't *prove* that truth is only what can be proved. And it's not perfectly clear that all truth is perfectly clear. In fact, many truths *cannot* be proved: for instance, the law of noncontradiction (X does not equal non-X). This is presupposed in all proofs, so that trying to prove it always begs the question; it assumes what you claim to prove. Many important truths also are not clear: for instance, the truth that most people are both good and bad, mysteriously mixed; or that "life is worth living."

4. ***The coherence theory of truth:*** "Truth is not a relationship of correspondence between an idea and its external object, but the coherence or oneness or harmony among a set of ideas." Truth is a consistency, wholeness or totality of ideas.

   The coherence theory presupposes the truth of something like the correspondence theory. For it claims it is true, that is, that this theory (coherence) really tells what is—or corresponds to the facts, the real situation, the way it really is—and that the other theory (correspondence) does not. Thus it contradicts itself. The coherence theory is incoherent.

All theories of truth, once they are expressed clearly and simply, presuppose the commonsensical notion of truth that is enshrined in the wisdom of language and the tradition of usage, namely the correspondence (or identity) theory. For each theory claims that it is really true, that is, that it corresponds to reality, and that the others are really false, that is, that they fail to correspond to reality.

Universal Subjectivism

Universal subjectivism claims that all truth is subjective, that is, "in" or dependent on the knower. This is self-contradictory. The contradiction lies in the fact that the subjectivist claims that truth really, objectively, *is* subjective. If they claimed only that the subjectivity of truth is a subjective truth, a mere personal opinion or feeling in the mind of the subjectivist, then they would not be claiming that the subjectivist theory was really correct and the objectivist theory incorrect. In that case they would not really be disagreeing with their opponents at all.

The subjectivist is the opposite error from the skeptic. The skeptic says there is truth for nobody. The subjectivist says there is truth for everybody. The skeptic denies truth; the subjectivist denies error. To a subjectivist, everything is true "for" somebody; for *truth* means "true for me" but not necessarily "true for you," because the link between "true for me" and "true for you," namely universal objective truth, is missing.

But if truth is only subjective, only true for me but not for you, then that truth too—the "truth" of subjectivism—is not true, but only "true for me," (i.e., true for the subjectivist). So the subjectivist is not saying that subjectivism is really true and objectivism really false, or that the objectivist is mistaken at all. He is not challenging his opponent, not arguing, not debating, only "sharing his feelings." "I feel well" does not contradict or refute *your* statement "I feel sick." Subjectivism is not an "ism," not a philosophy. It does not rise to the level of deserving our attention or refutation. Its claim is like "I itch," not "I know."

Religious Subjectivism

Religious subjectivism is a very popular position today. It sees not *all* truth, but the truth of religion as "true for you but not for me." This really means that it sees religious truth as feeling, or a mode of sensibility, or something to help us cope and live more successfully, or a set of ideals and values, rather than as a creed, as statements that are either true or false because they claim to reveal facts, like "Christ has died; Christ is risen; Christ will come again."

Religion does include all these other dimensions, but it also claims to include fact-claims (e.g., that one all-powerful, all-good and all-knowing God exists; that he created the universe; that he became a man and died and rose; that there is a real, objective moral law; and that there is a real judgment, a real heaven and a real hell). These claims may be true or they may be false, but they are not claims about things inside our consciousness but about things outside it. They are about objective truth, not subjective truth; about beings, not just consciousness; about laws, not just values; about the resurrection of a real man of flesh and blood, not about the mere arising of "Easter faith" in people's minds.

Religious subjectivism really means religion is made by us, dependent on us, "true" only as a fantasy is "true." This is a polite way of saying that God is just an adult version of Santa Claus and that religious believers are just adults who never grew up.

The claim is too sweeping and vague to be fair. It cannot even be argued about until it becomes specific. It is like the claim that "science" has disproved "religion." The reply has to be, Which science? Which discovery? By whom? When? What is the proof of it? Which religion? Which doctrine? What does this doctrine really mean, really claim? And are these two truth-claims then logically contradictory or not?

As we suggested above (in chapter two, on faith and reason, and in chapter six, on miracles), each specific challenge can be refuted. There are no contradictions between science and religion. The natural laws of physics do not refute supernatural miracles. Evolution does not refute creation. Each specific contradiction claim can be answered. What is left is a vague, general ideology or prejudice that "science" contradicts "religion."

The claim that religious truth is "subjective" is in exactly the same situation. Once it becomes specific, it can be answered. For instance, the claim that Christ's resurrection was not an objective fact but a subjective fable can be refuted by argument and evidence (see chapter nine). The claim that "God" is only "all the good in humanity" can be refuted by proving the existence of an objective God (chapter three).

Conclusion

The Bottom Line

Whoever you are, you who are reading this book, you are either (1) a Christian—in which case you are reading this book not to find out whether Christianity is true or false but to try to understand it better and to learn how to argue for it and persuade others of its truth; or (2) not a Christian—in which case you are probably reading this book out of curiosity, to find out why Christians believe the things they believe and also, we hope, out of an honest search for truth, an open-minded wondering whether this thing is really true after all.

The following remarks about the search for truth are addressed to both categories of people. Believers can interpret these remarks as practical battle plans, for they have already chosen sides. Nonbelievers can interpret them as a travel agent's layout of the stages ahead on the Christian road, what travelers who choose to go further down this road will be in for.

We must distinguish four steps in becoming a Christian.

The first step is mental belief. This is first because you cannot take any other step toward a goal unless you believe it exists. You cannot seek or deal with a Person you do not believe exists. You cannot pray to a God you think is dead.

The next three steps are (2) repentance from sin; (3) saving faith, faith in a more than mental sense, acceptance of Christ as Savior; and (4) living out the Christian life. These three steps all presuppose the truth of the God to whom you repent, in whom you believe and with whose real presence and help you now live.

This book is designed to persuade you to take that first step, if you have not already taken it, by means of rational arguments. If you have taken that step and believe Christianity is true, this book is designed to help you to persuade others to take that first step.

But that first step is a mere beginning. Much, much more is in store for the believer. The first step is like believing in the accuracy of a road map; the next three steps are like actually using the map.

Even for step one, the intellect alone is not enough. The will has a necessary part to play too. For no one *will* believe unless they are *willing* to believe. This does not necessarily mean prejudice. It takes the will to open the mind as well as to close it. You do not need a positive push or predilection for Christianity, but you do need a positive predilection for objective truth wherever it may be found. No, stronger than a predilection, you need a definite, deliberate choice to love and seek and find and know the truth wherever it is.

This claim—that all seekers find—is testable by experience, by experiment. If you are an honest scientist, here is a way to find out whether Christianity is true or not. Perform the relevant experiment. To test the hypothesis that someone is behind the door, knock. To test the Christian hypothesis that Christ is behind the door, knock.

How do you knock? Pray! Tell Christ you are seeking the truth—seeking *him*, if he is the truth. Ask him to fulfill his promise that all who seek him will find him—in his own time, of course. He promised that you would find, but he didn't promise a schedule. He's a lover, not a train.

But, you may reply, I don't know whether Christ is God; I don't even know whether there is a God. That's all right; you can pray the prayer of the skeptic:

> God, I don't know whether you even exist. I'm a skeptic. I doubt. I think you may be only a myth. But I'm not certain (at least not when I'm completely honest with myself). So if you do exist, and if you really did promise to reward all seekers, you must be hearing me now. So I hereby declare myself a seeker, a seeker of the truth, whatever it is and wherever it is. I want to know the truth and live the truth. If you are the truth, please help me.

If Christianity is true, he will. Such a prayer constitutes a scientifically fair test of the Christian "hypothesis"—that is, if you do not put unfair restrictions on God, like demanding a miracle (your way, not his) or certainty by tomorrow (your time, not his). The demand that God act like your servant is hardly a scientifically fair test of the hypothesis that there is a God who is your King.

But all this King asks for at first is honesty, not faking a faith you do not have. Honesty is a choice of the will—the choice to seek the truth no matter what or where. This is the most momentous choice you can make. It is the choice of light over darkness, ultimately heaven over hell.

Honesty is infinitely more momentous than we often think. It is also much harder than we think. Our culture trivializes honesty into merely "sharing your feelings," telling others about the state of your nerve endings. That's not the opposite of dishonesty, it's just the opposite of shame, or shyness. Shallow honesty seeks "sharing"; deep honesty seeks truth. Shallow honesty stands in the presence of others; deep honesty stands in the presence of God.

Works Cited

Craig, William Lane. *Knowing the Truth About the Resurrection.* Ann Arbor, Mich.: Servant, 1988.

Lewis, C. S. "The Poison of Subjectivism." In *Christian Reflections.* Edited by Walter Hooper. Grand Rapids: Eerdmans, 1967.

———. *The Great Divorce.* New York: Simon & Schuster, 1996.

———. *Mere Christianity.* Revised edition. San Francisco: HarperSanFrancisco, 2001.

———. *The Problem of Pain.* San Francisco: HarperSanFrancisco, 2001.

Pascal, *Pensées.* Translated by A. J. Krailsheimer. London: Penguin, 1988.

Purtill, R. L. *Thinking About Religion.* Englewood Cliffs, N.J.: Prentice Hall, 1978.

Thomas Aquinas. *Summa Contra Gentiles.* 5 vols. Notre Dame, Ind.: University of Notre Dame Press, 1975.

Pocket Reference Collection from IVP Academic

Pocket Dictionary for the Study of Biblical Hebrew
by Todd J. Murphy, 183 pages, 1458-9

Pocket Dictionary for the Study of New Testament Greek
by Matthew S. DeMoss, 138 pages, 1464-0

Pocket Dictionary of Apologetics & Philosophy of Religion
by C. Stephen Evans, 125 pages, 1465-7

Pocket Dictionary of Biblical Studies
by Arthur G. Patzia and Anthony J. Petrotta, 128 pages, 1467-1

Pocket Dictionary of Church History
by Nathan P. Feldmeth, 144 pages, 2703-9

Pocket Dictionary of Ethics
by Stanley J. Grenz and Jay T. Smith, 128 pages, 1468-8

Pocket Dictionary of New Religious Movements
by Irving Hexham, 120 pages, 1466-4

Pocket Dictionary of North American Denominations
by Drew Blankman and Todd Augustine, 144 pages, 1459-6

Pocket Dictionary of Theological Terms
by Stanley J. Grenz, David Guretzki and Cherith Fee Nordling, 122 pages, 1449-7

Pocket Guide to World Religions
by Winfried Corduan, 144 pages, 2705-3

Pocket Handbook of Christian Apologetics
by Peter Kreeft and Ronald K. Tacelli, 142 pages, 2702-2

Pocket History of Evangelical Theology
by Roger E. Olson, 151 pages, 2706-0

Pocket History of the Church
by D. Jeffrey Bingham, 192 pages, 2701-5

Pocket History of Theology
by Roger E. Olson and Adam C. English, 112 pages, 2704-6

InterVarsity Press
Downers Grove, Illinois 60515
ivpress.com